ART DECO and GEOMETRIC
Stained Glass Pattern Book

Richard Welch and Hollis Welch

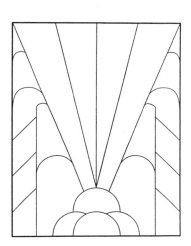

DOVER PUBLICATIONS, INC.
Mineola, New York

Copyright

Copyright © 1997 by Dover Publications, Inc.
All rights reserved under Pan American and International Copyright Conventions.

Published in Canada by General Publishing Company, Ltd., 30 Lesmill Road, Don Mills, Toronto, Ontario.
Published in the United Kingdom by Constable and Company, Ltd., 3 The Lanchesters, 162–164 Fulham Palace Road, London W6 9ER.

Bibliographical Note

Art Deco and Geometric Stained Glass Pattern Book is a new work, first published by Dover Publications, Inc., in 1997.

DOVER *Pictorial Archive* SERIES

Library of Congress Cataloging-in-Publication Data

Welch, Richard.
    Art deco and geometric stained glass pattern book / Richard Welch and Hollis Welch.
        p.   cm.
    ISBN 0-486-29841-8 (pbk.)
    1. Glass crafts—Patterns. 2. Glass painting and staining—Patterns.
    3. Art deco. I. Welch, Hollis. II. Title.
TT298.W46   1997
748.5—dc21   97-22489
                                                                    CIP

Manufactured in the United States of America
Dover Publications, Inc., 31 East 2nd Street, Mineola, N.Y. 11501

Publisher's Note

The Art Deco style of the early 20th century was characterized by its application of sleek, geometric forms and highly stylized imagery to all aspects of decoration and design. Architecture, furniture, ironwork, jewelry, textiles, and graphic work were but a few of the mediums to reflect the movement's influence: stained glass design, which flourished during that period, proved especially receptive to Art Deco's use of intricate patterns and brilliant colors, the two-dimensional nature of the medium being perfectly suited to the geometry of the designs. Although Art Deco's prevalence waned after its heyday in the 1920s and 1930s, it never disappeared completely; the recent renewal of interest in this period among artists and designers demonstrates the continued validity of this style as a source of creative inspiration.

The 136 Art Deco and geometric designs rendered specially for this book will provide stained glass workers a host of ideas for their projects. The patterns—which include sunbursts, cruciforms, flowers, and landscapes, as well as more abstract motifs—can be used for mirrors, transoms, lightcatchers, windows, and many other applications. All of the figures can be enlarged or reduced as required, and all are copyright-free.

This book is ideal for use with stained glass instruction books (such as *Stained Glass Craft* by J. A. F. Divine and G. Blachford, Dover Publications, Inc., 0-486-22812-6), and may be used by novices and professionals alike. Suppliers of glass, general instructions, and other necessary materials should be listed under Hobbies or Crafts in your local Yellow Pages.

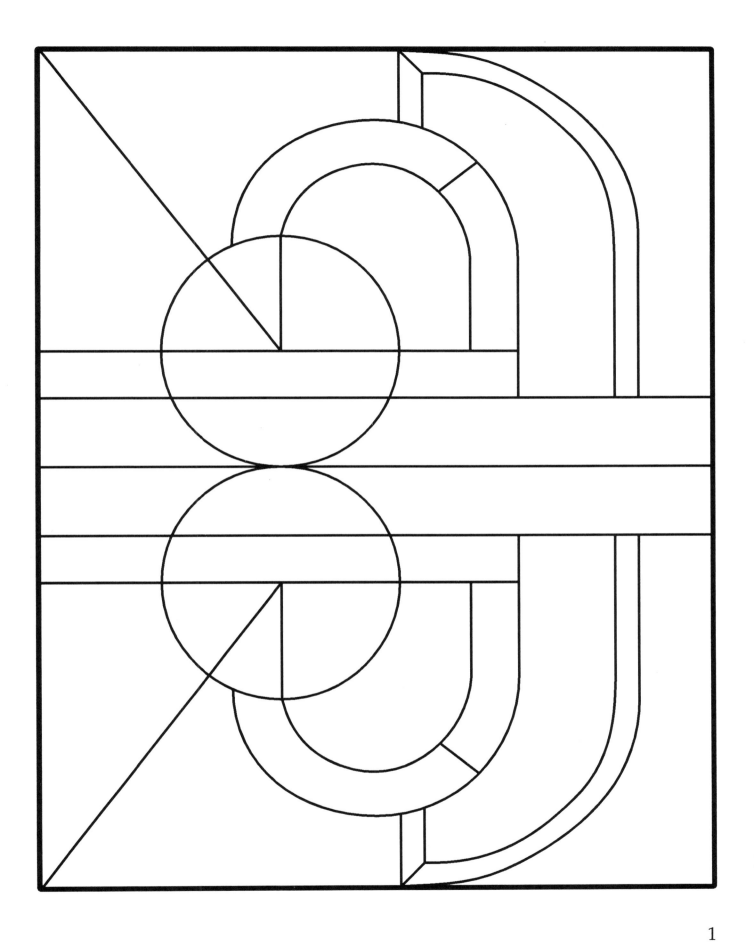

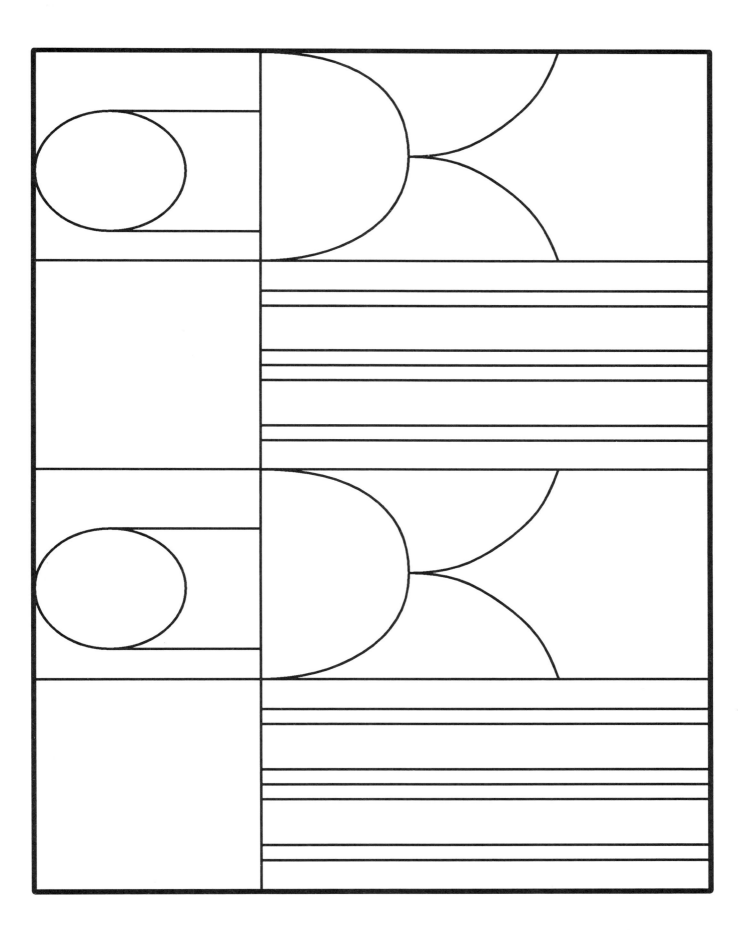

3

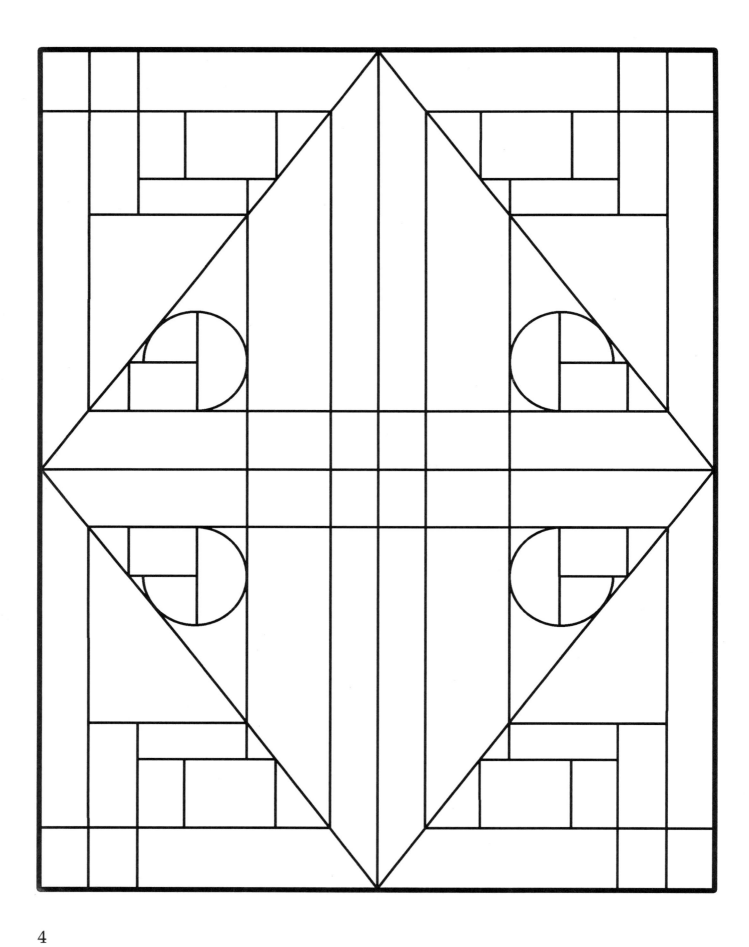

4

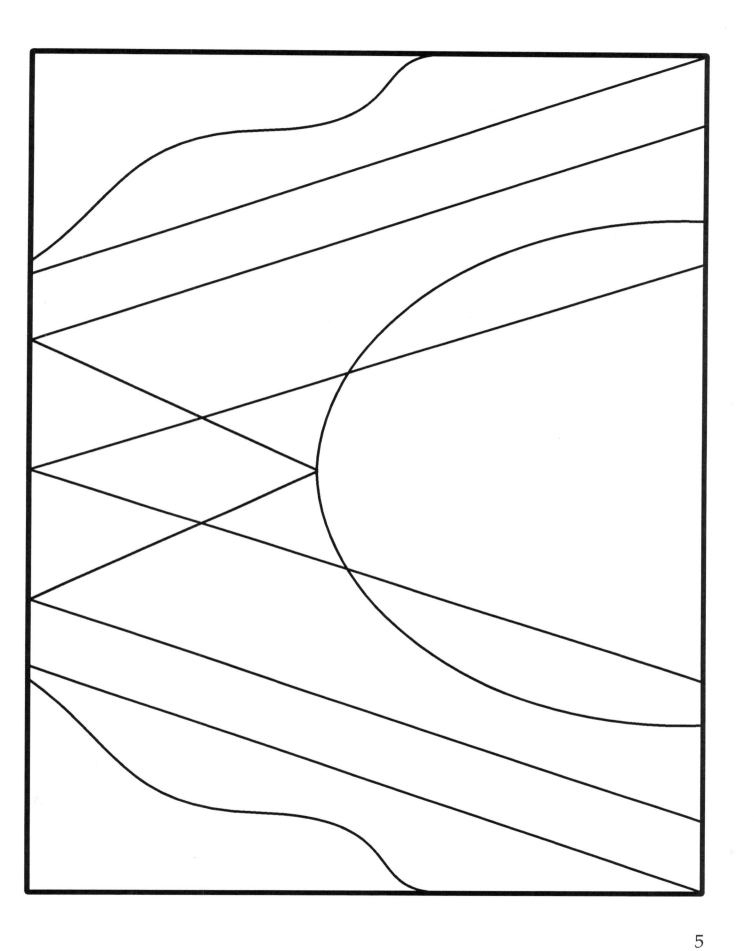

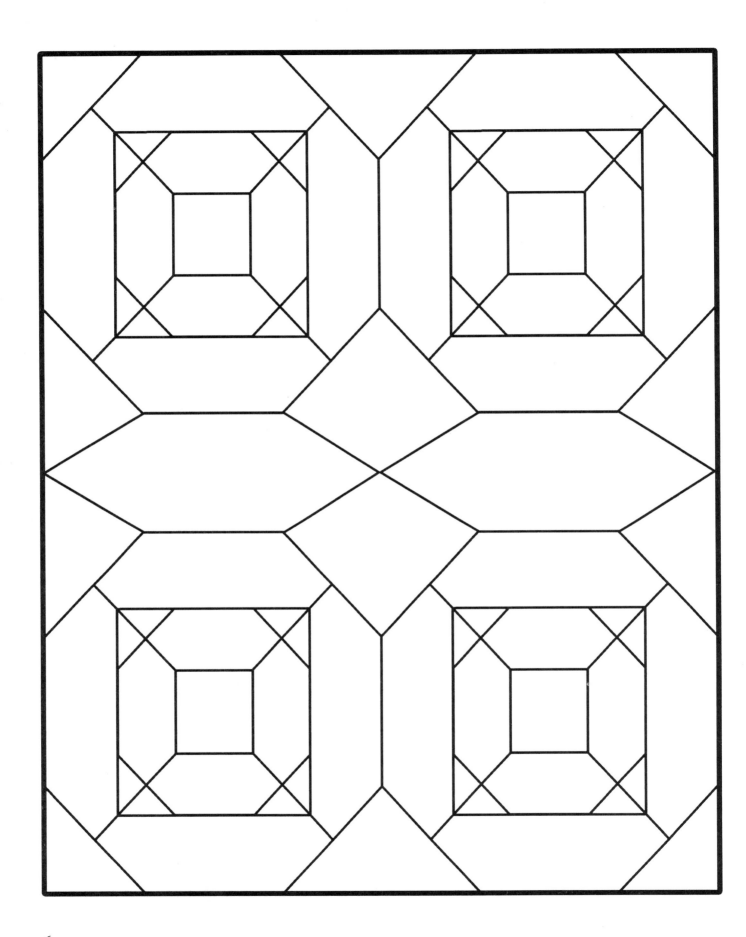

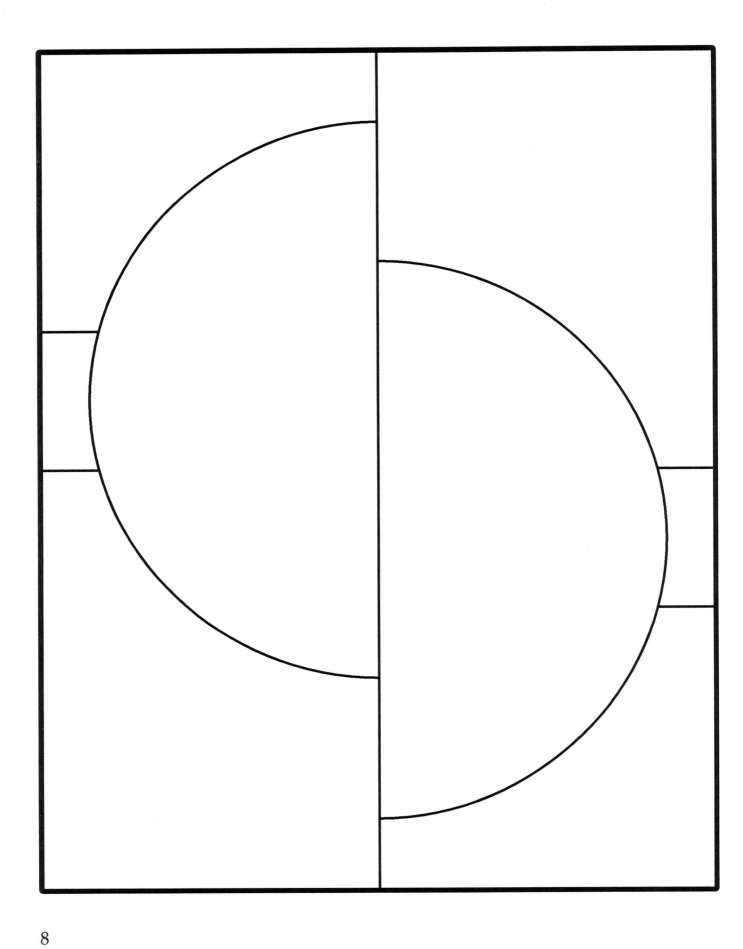

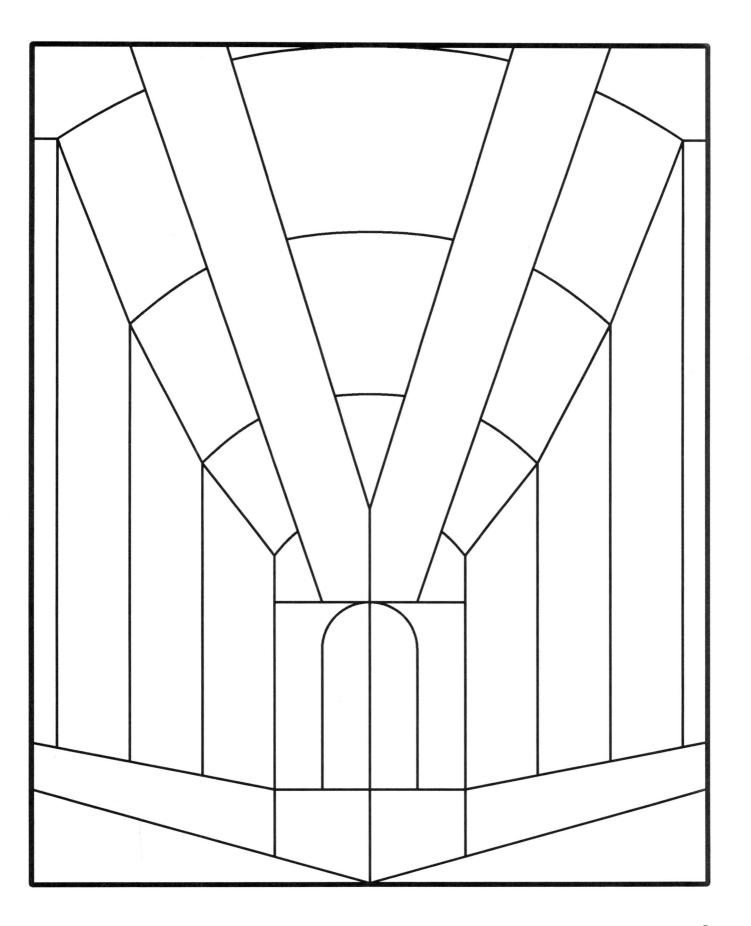

11

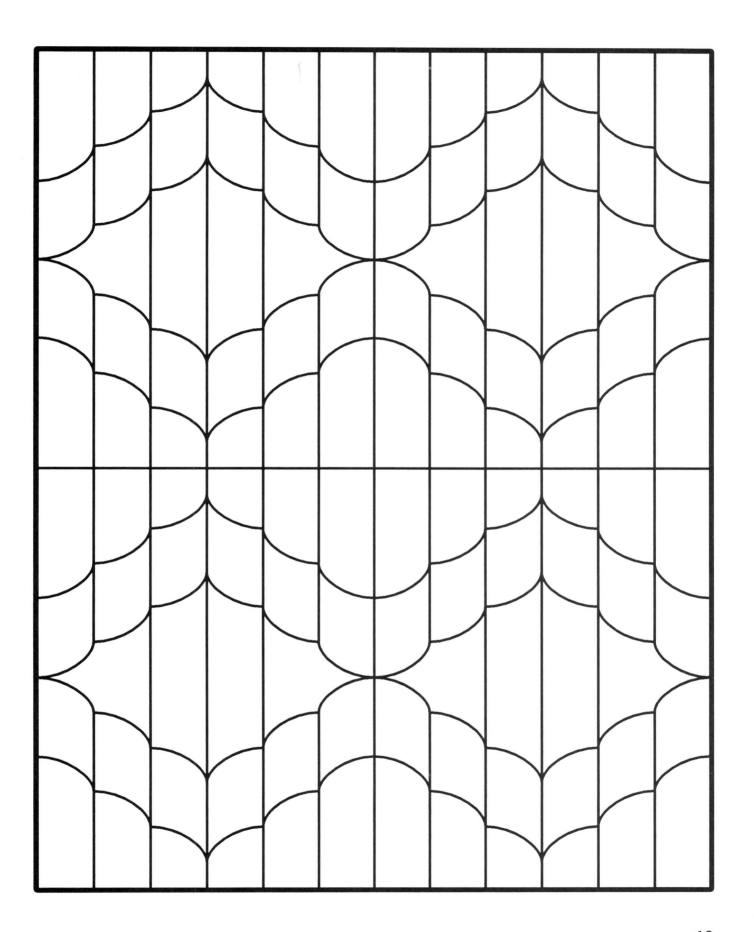

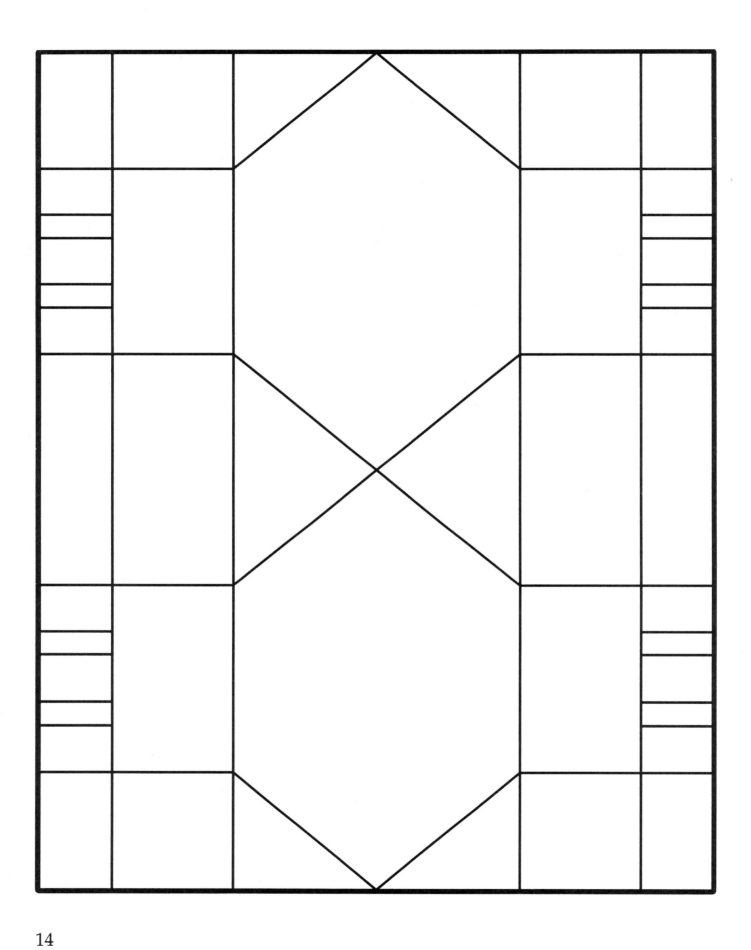

14

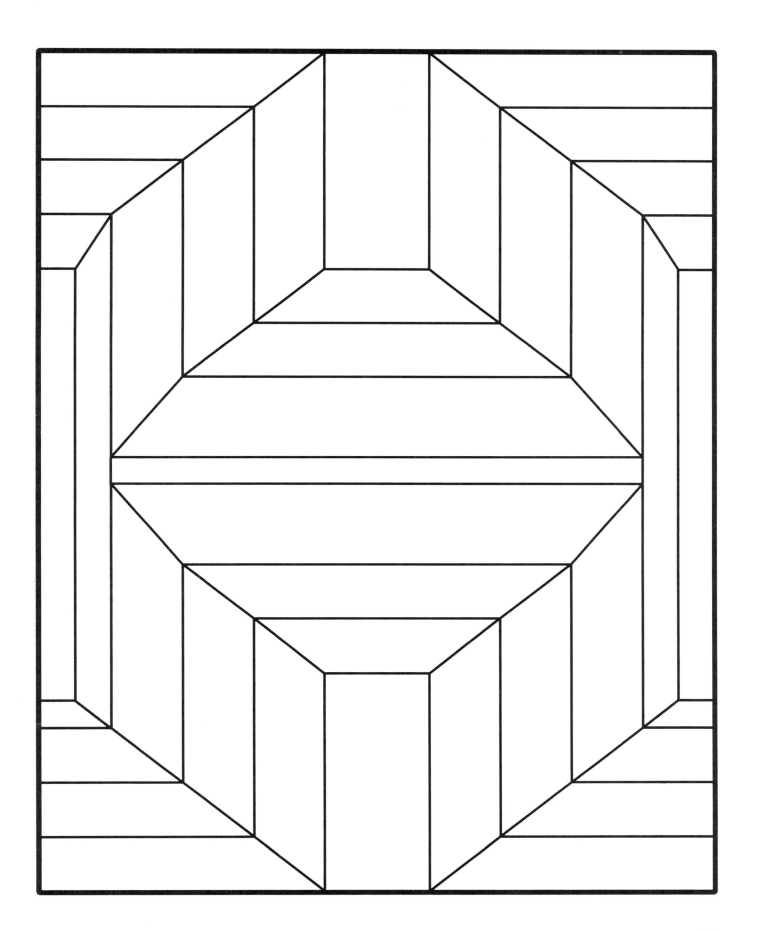

15

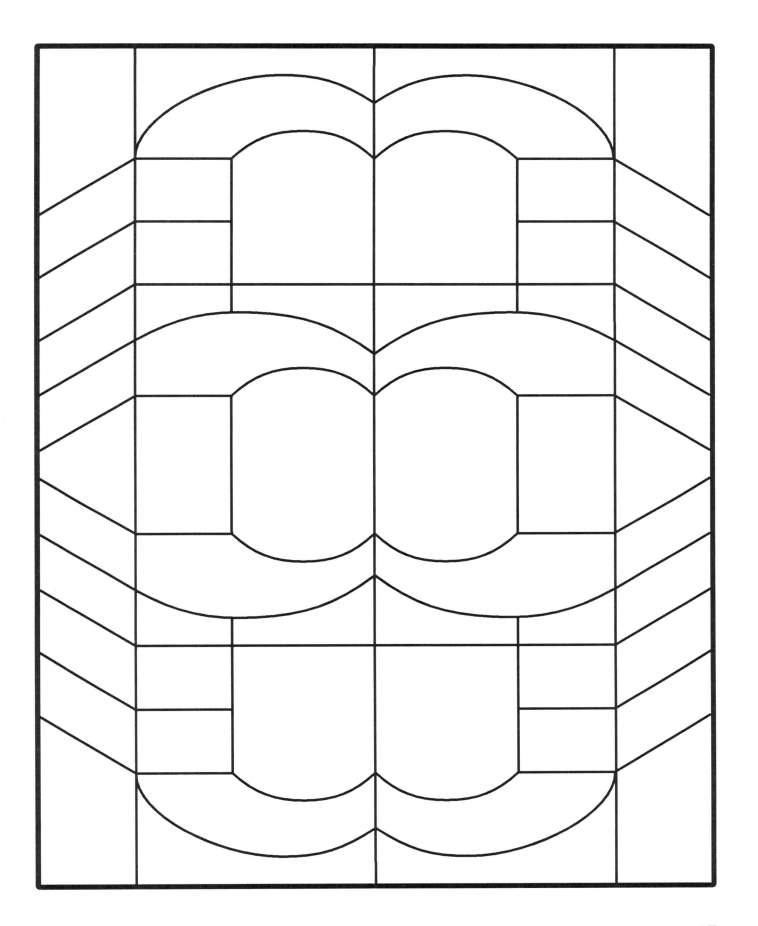

17

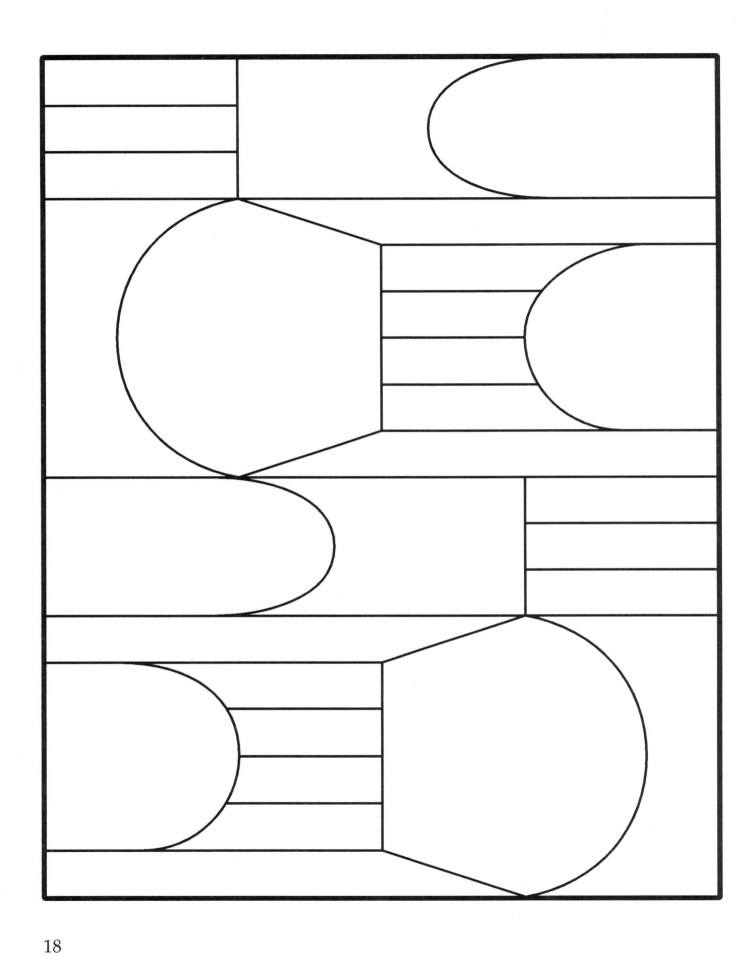

18

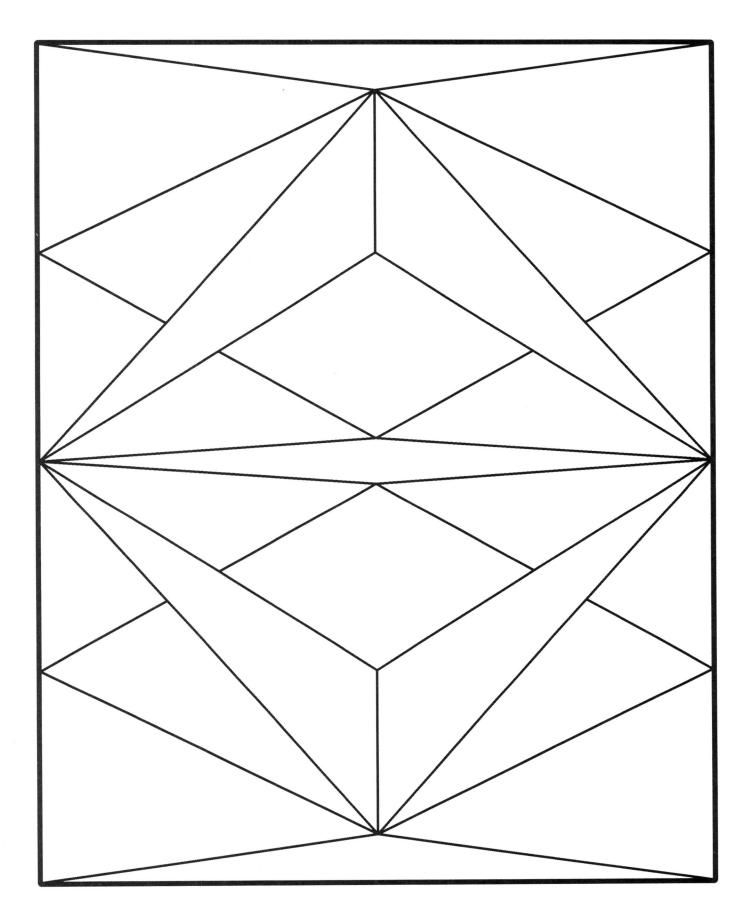

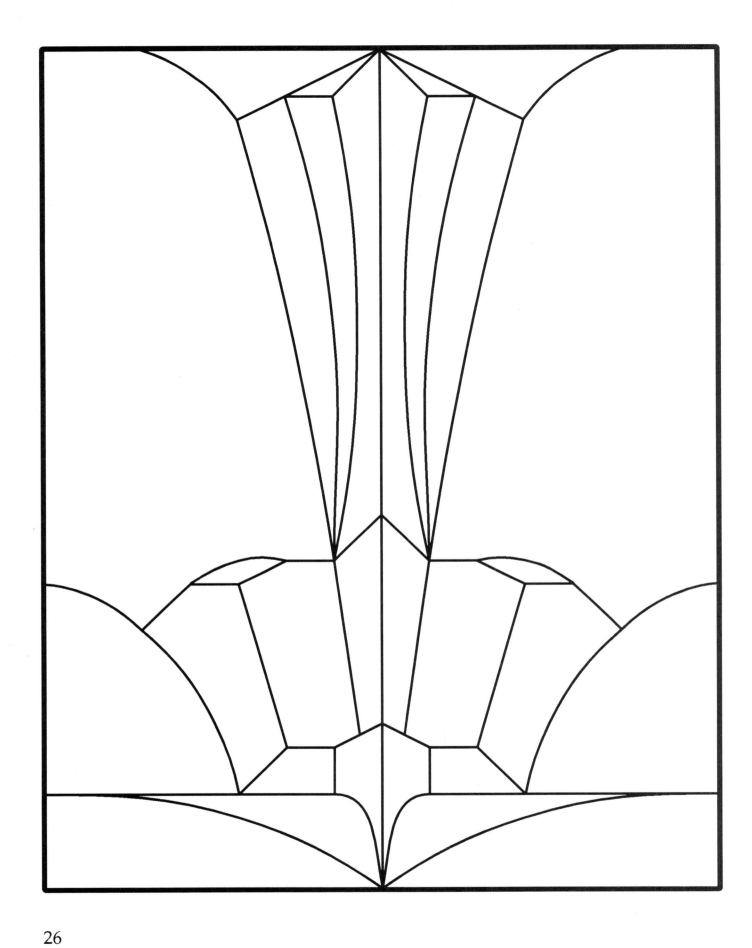

26

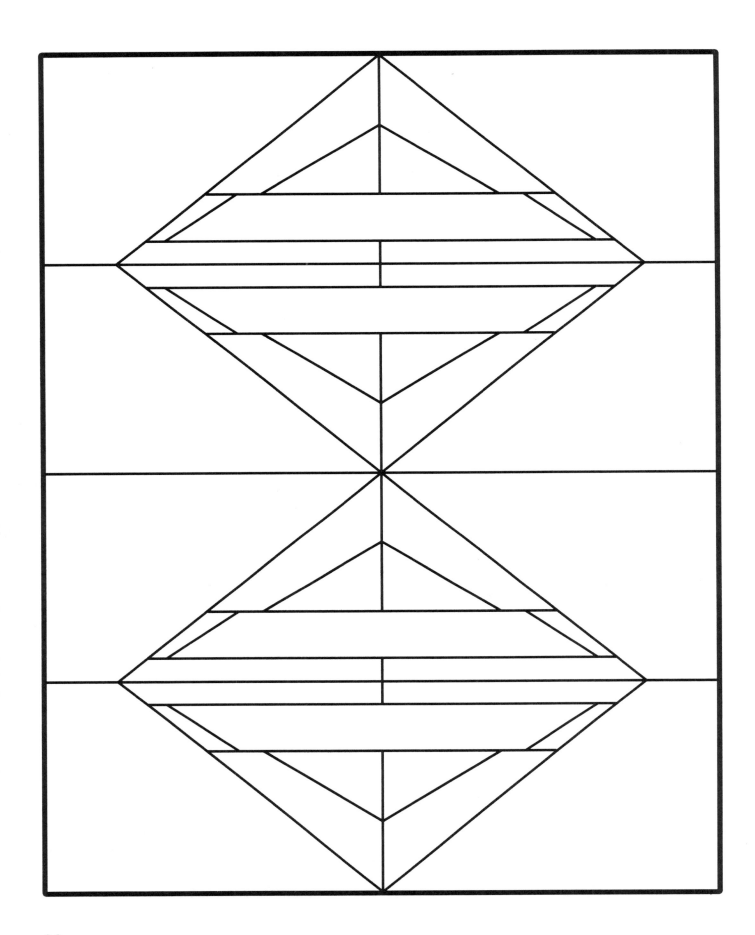

28

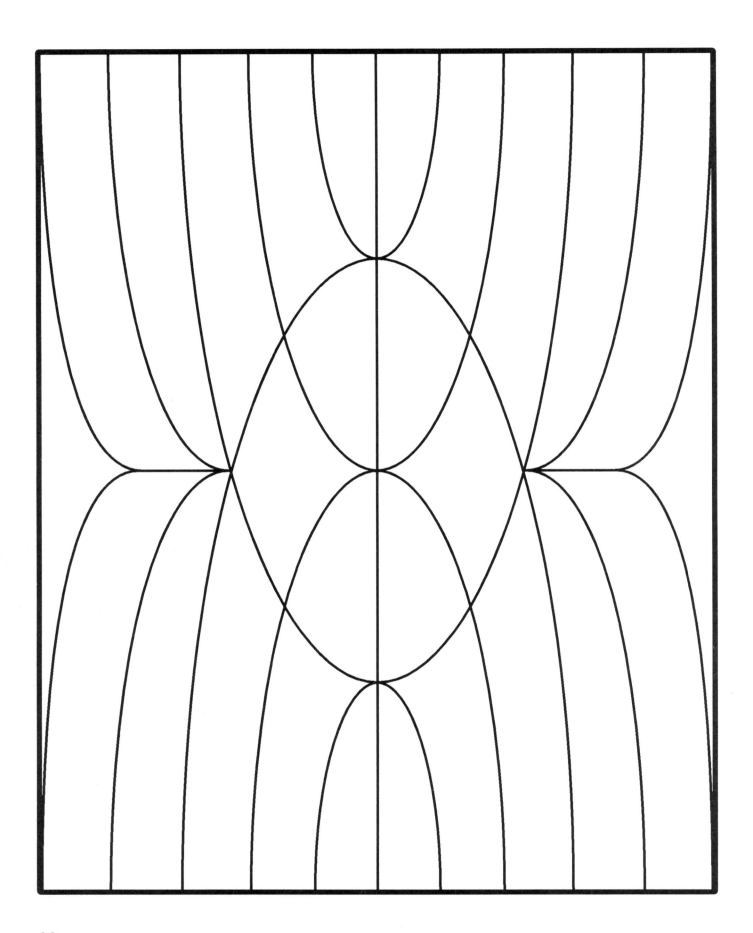

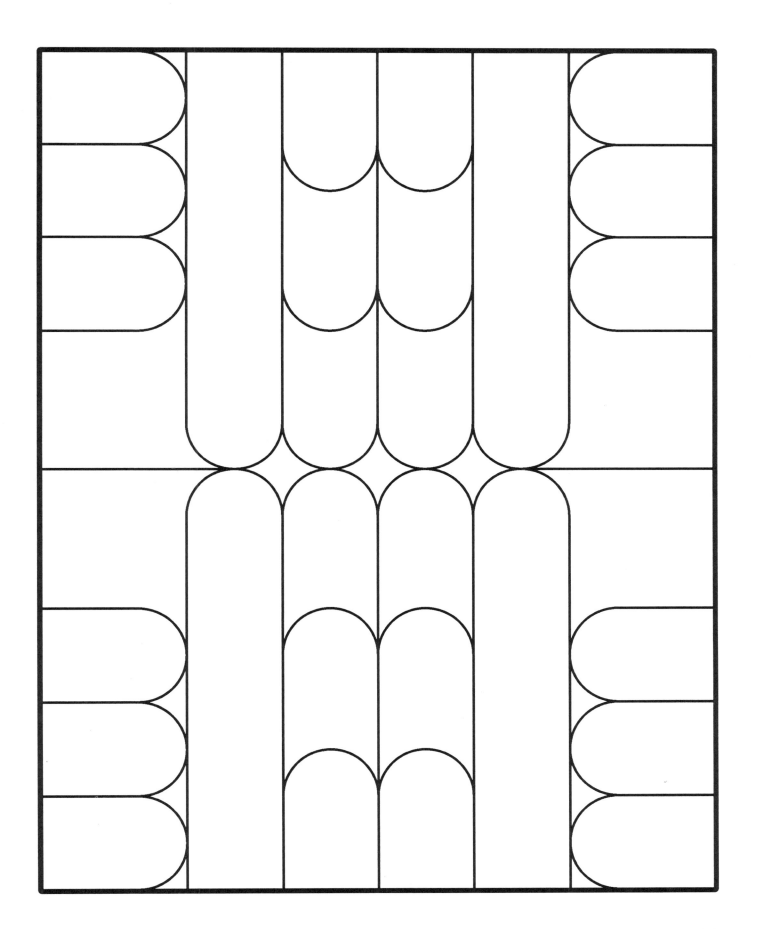

33

34

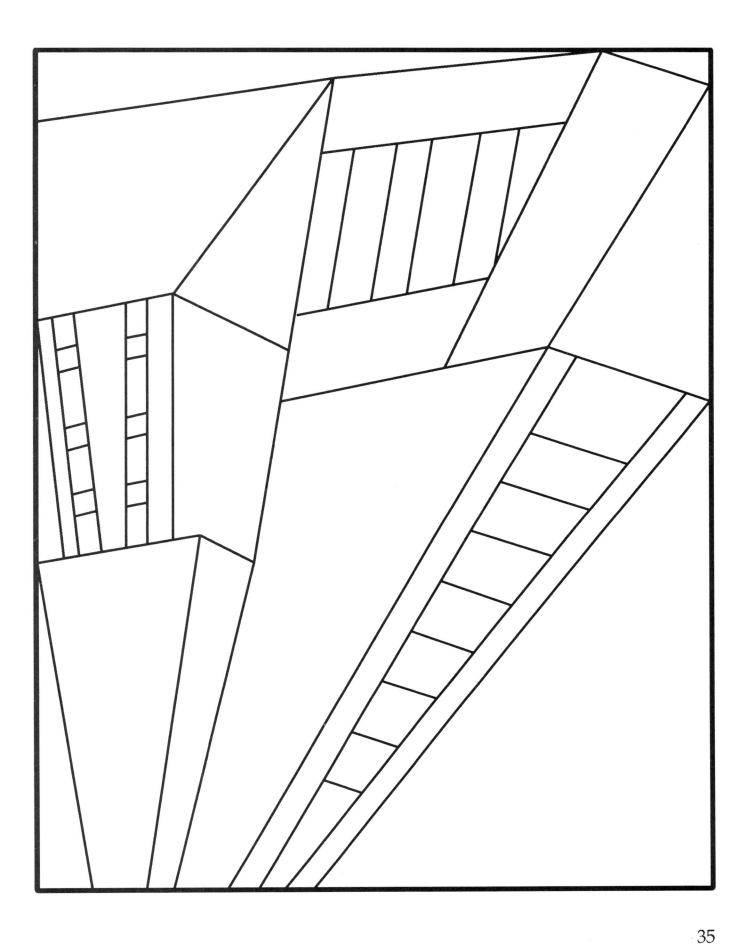

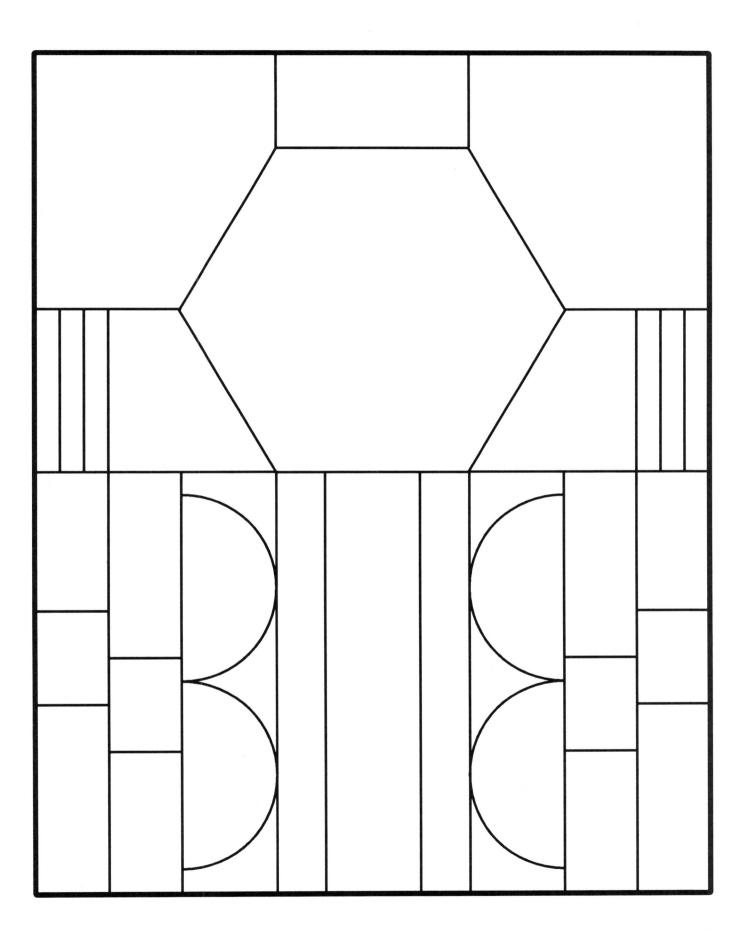

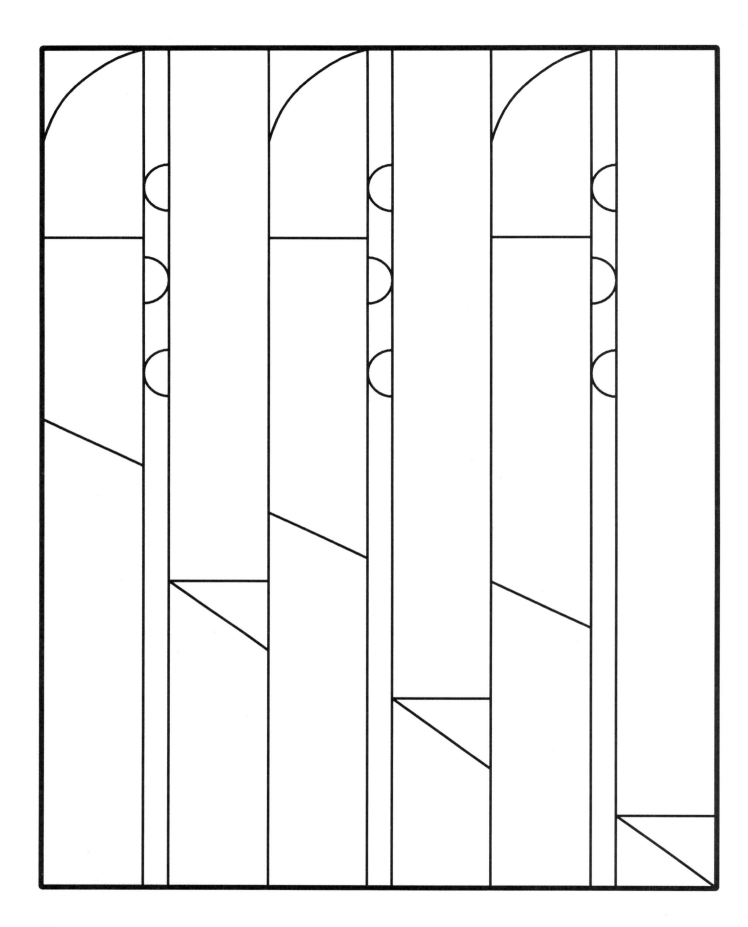

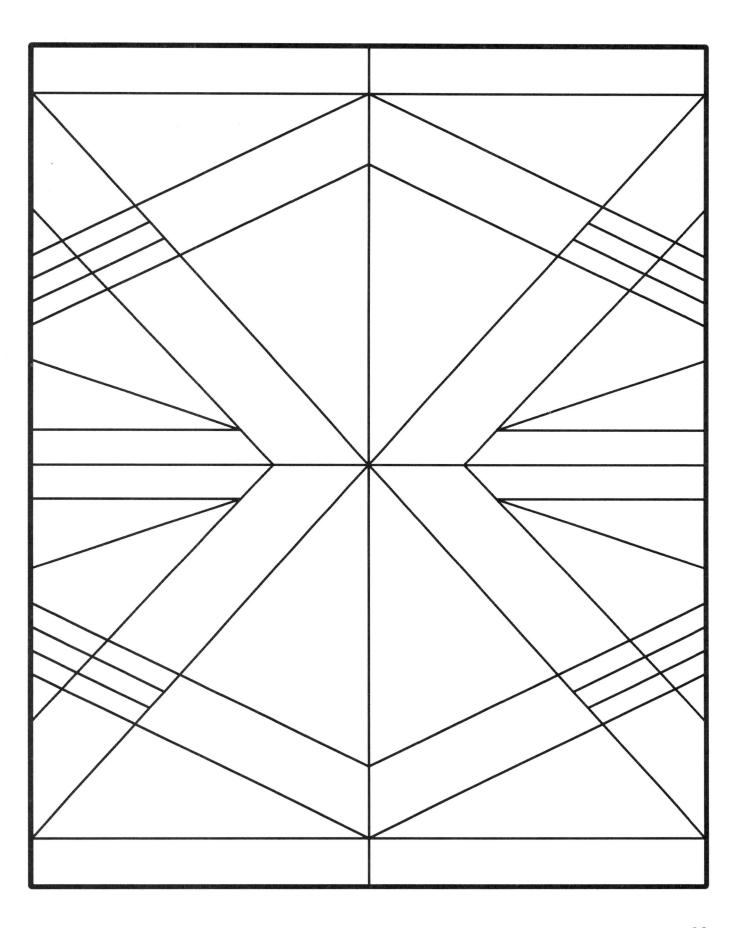

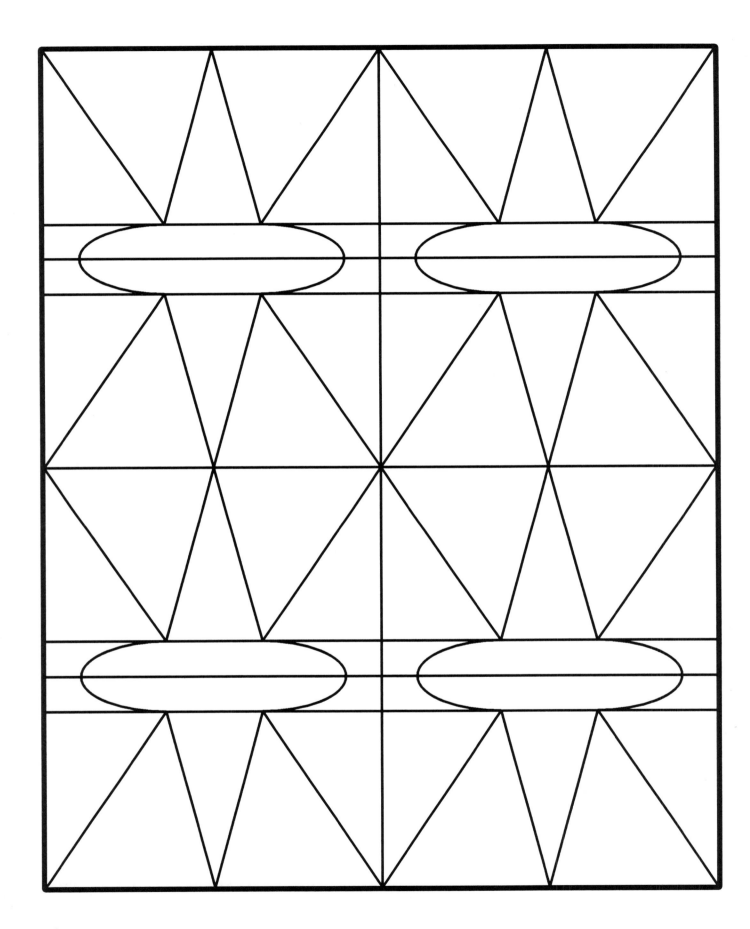

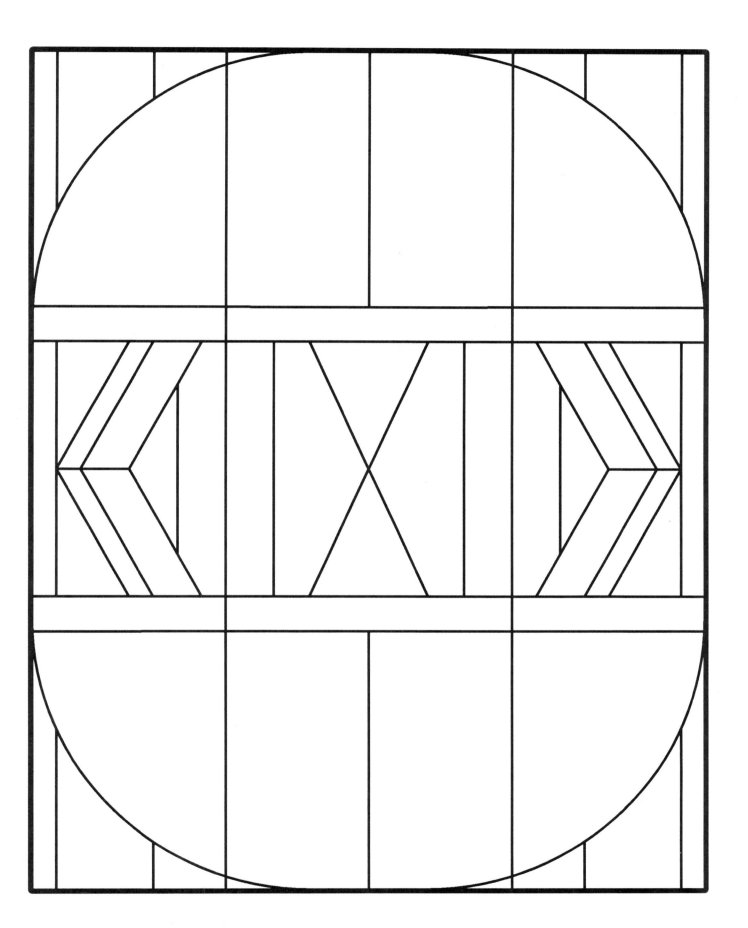

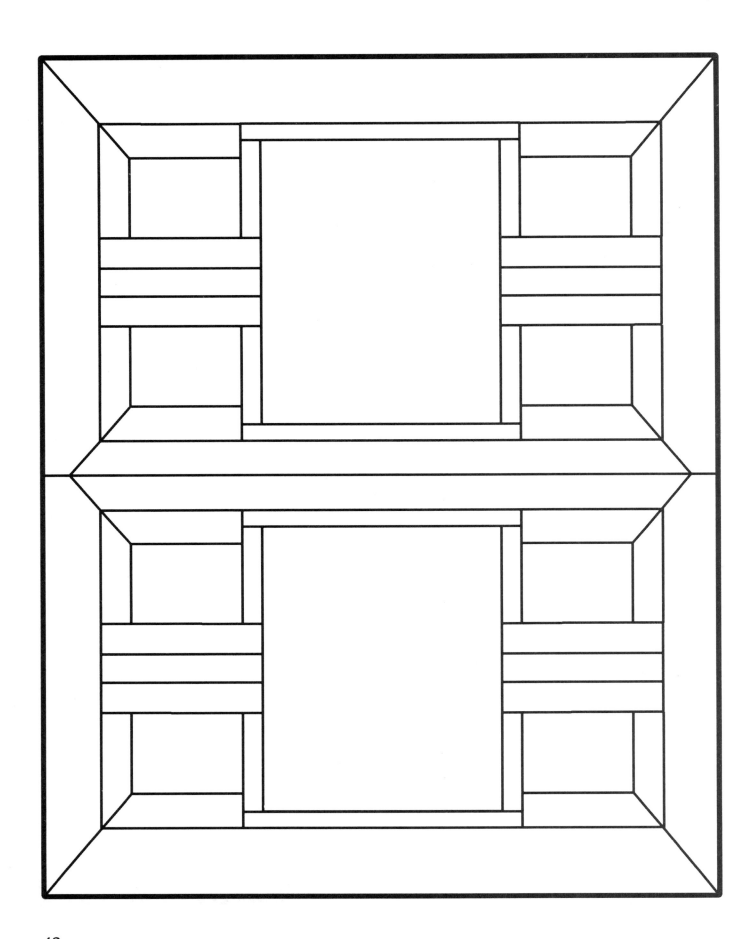

42

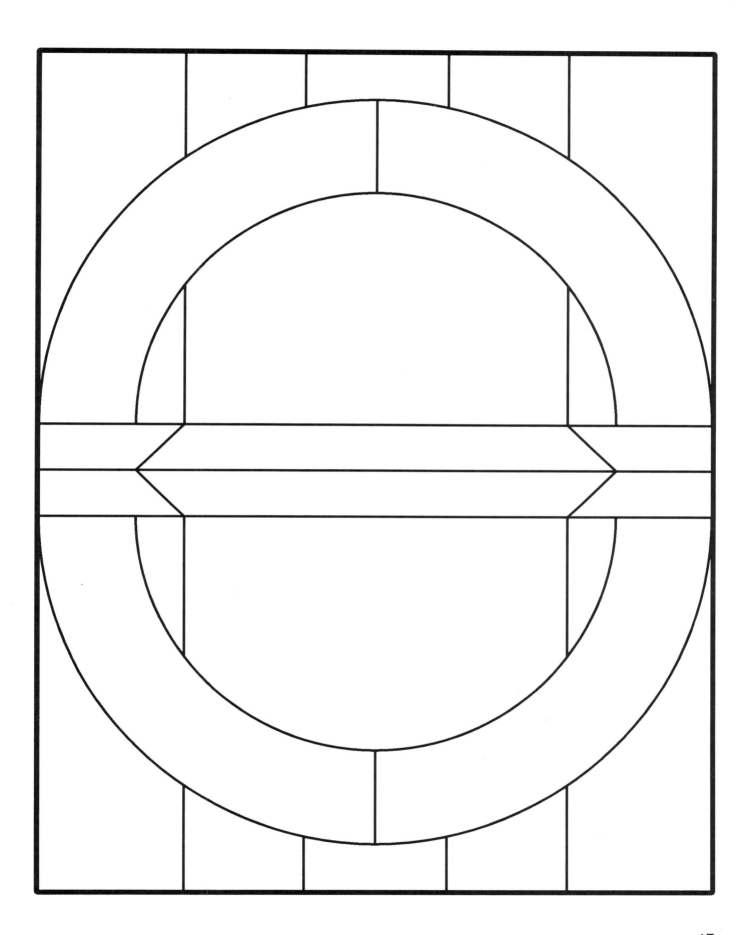

45

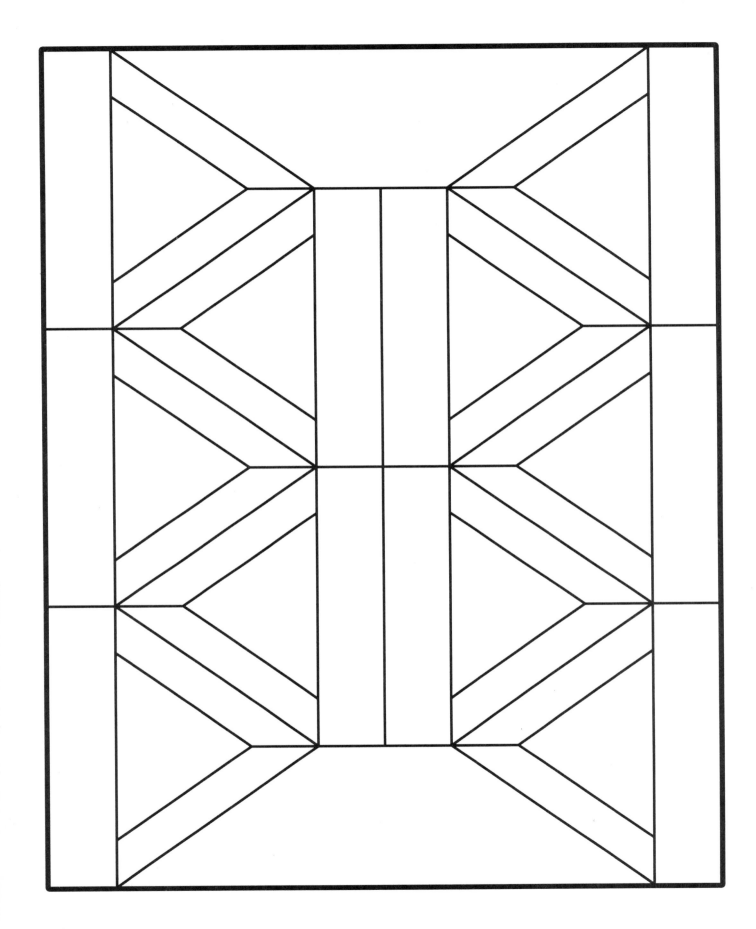

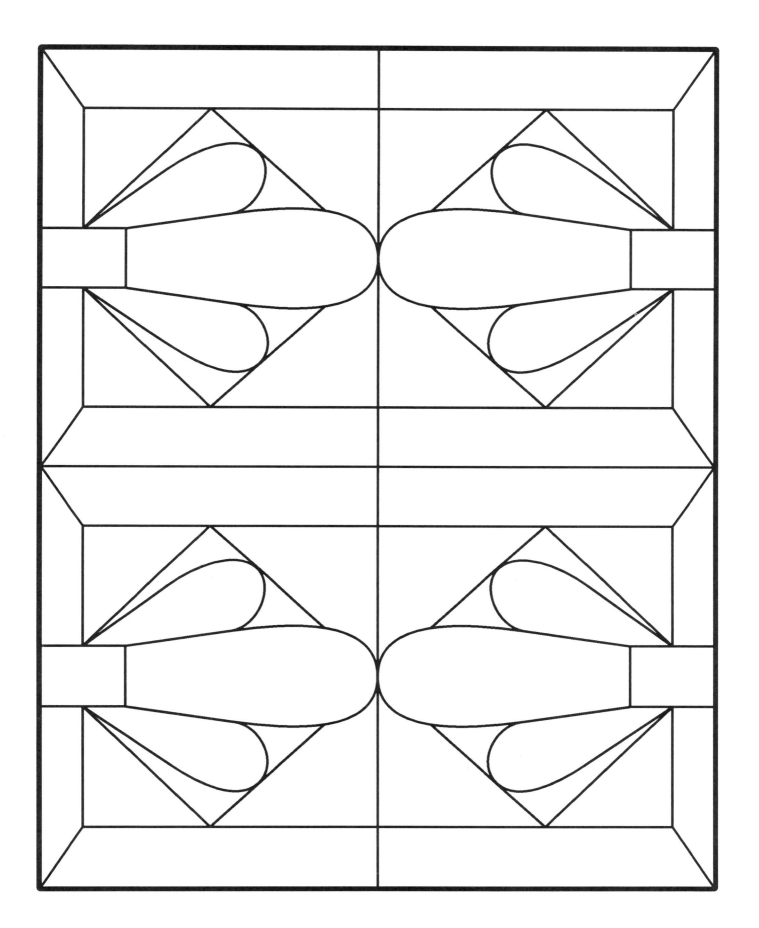

47

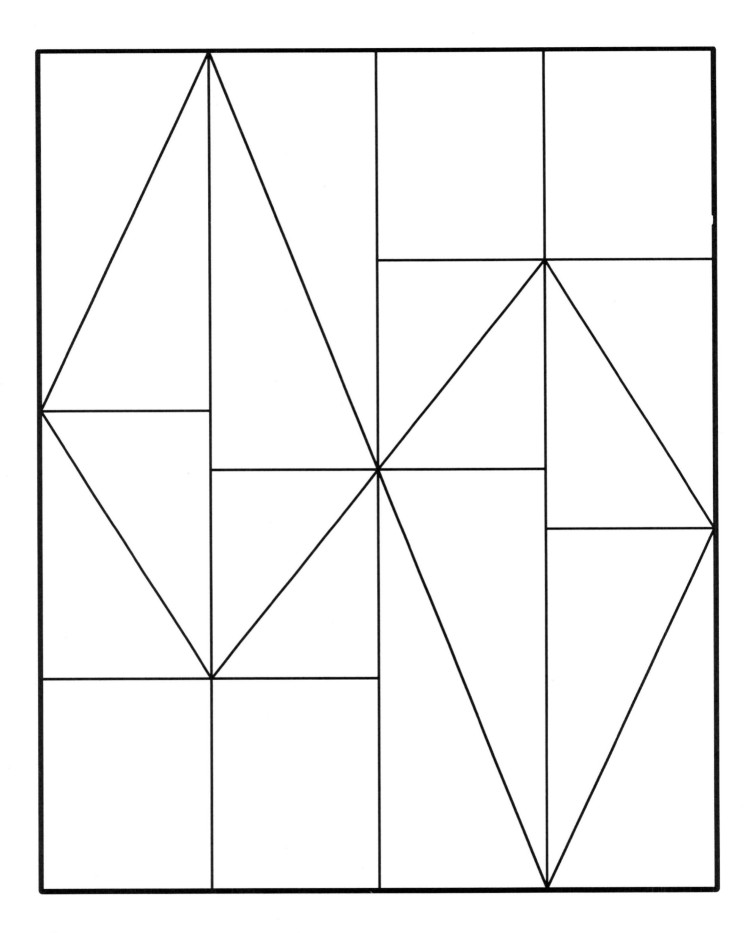

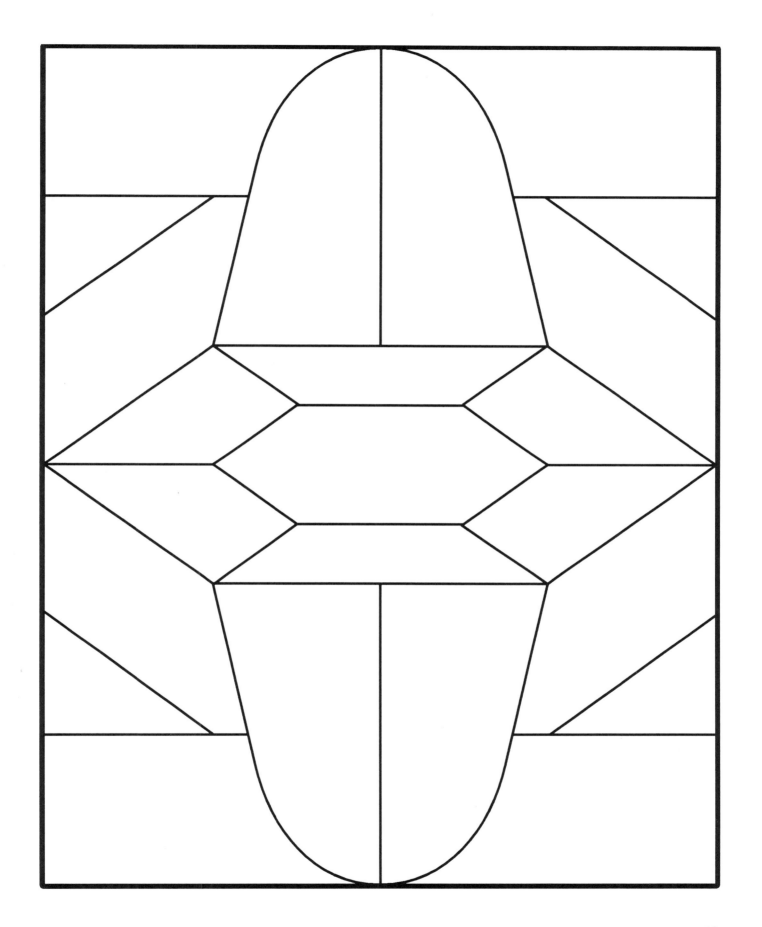

49

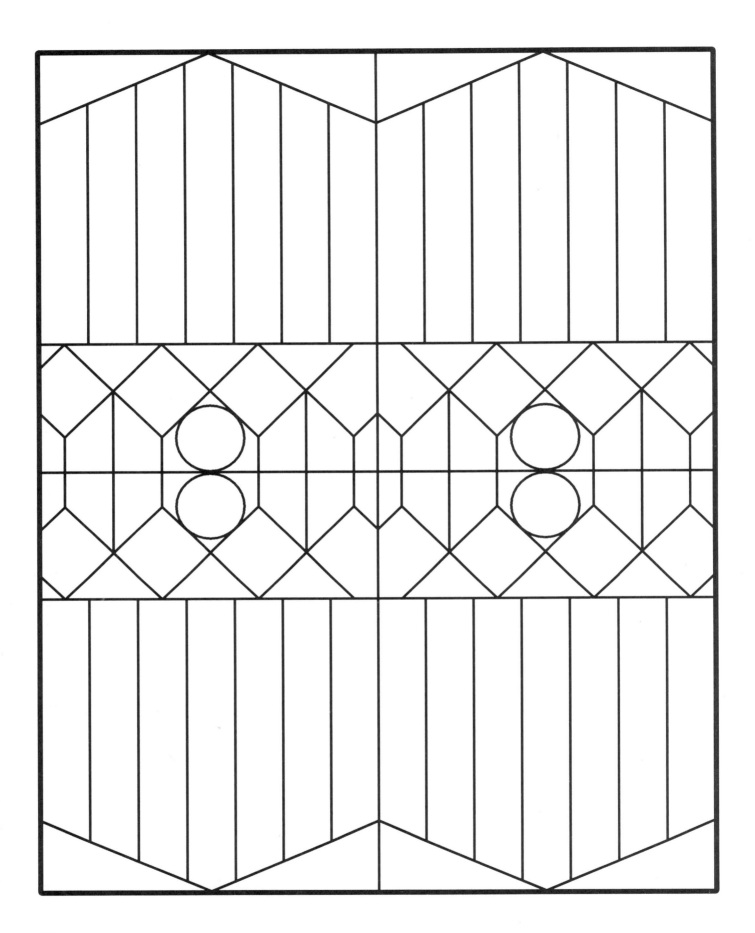

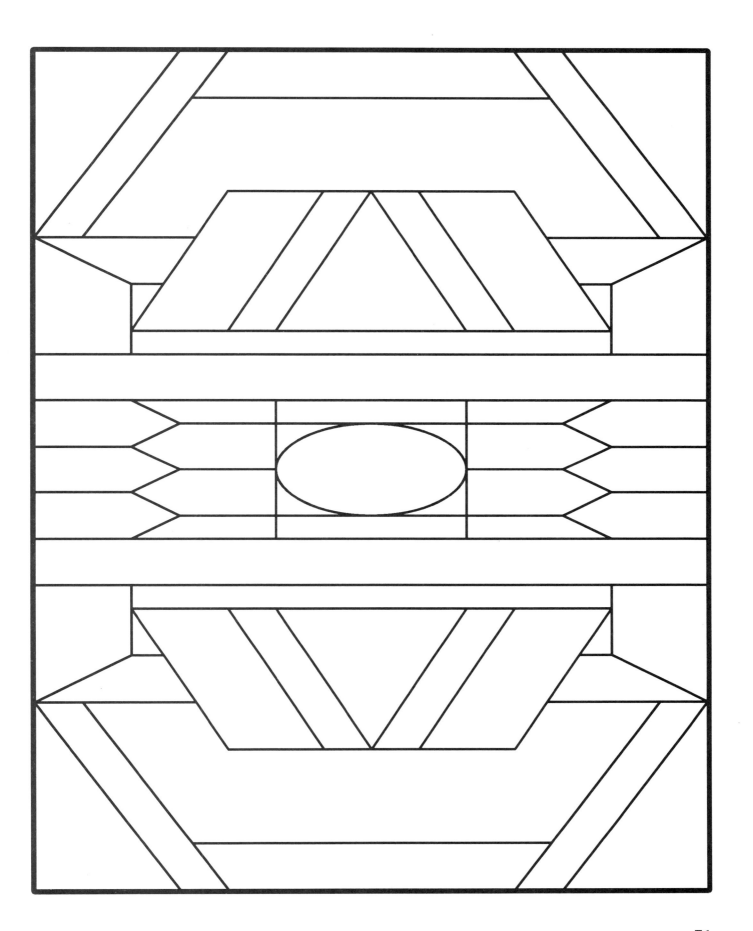

51

52

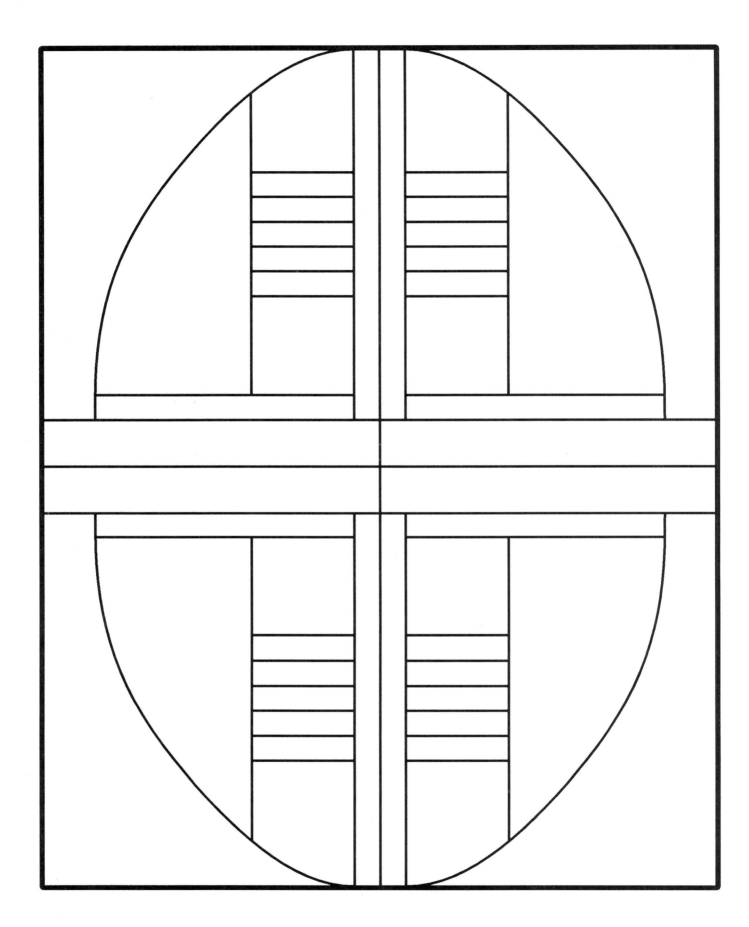

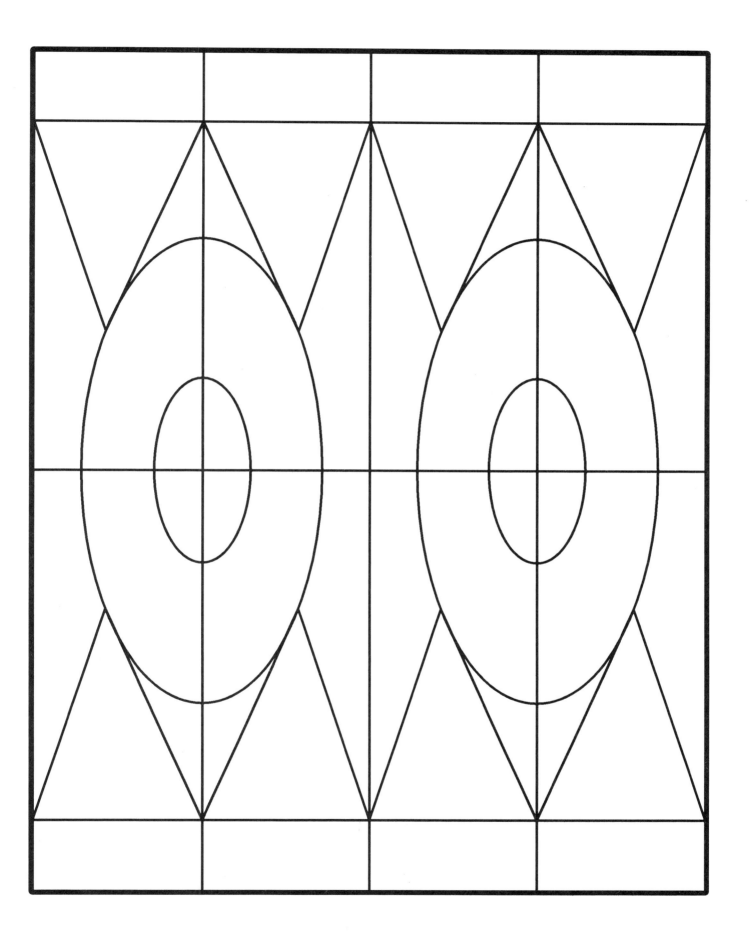

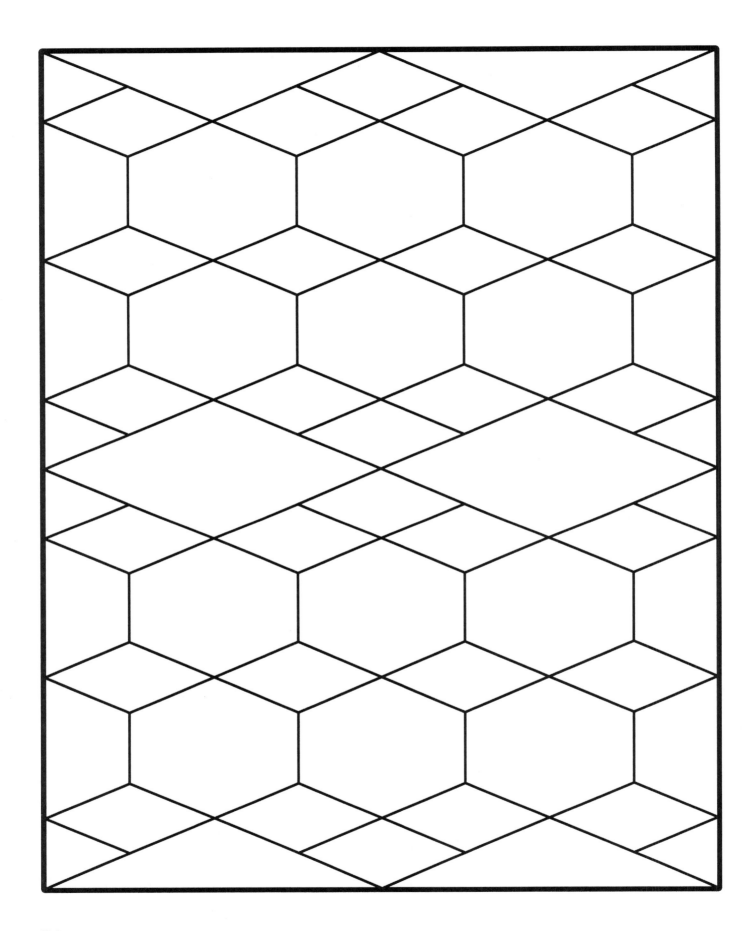

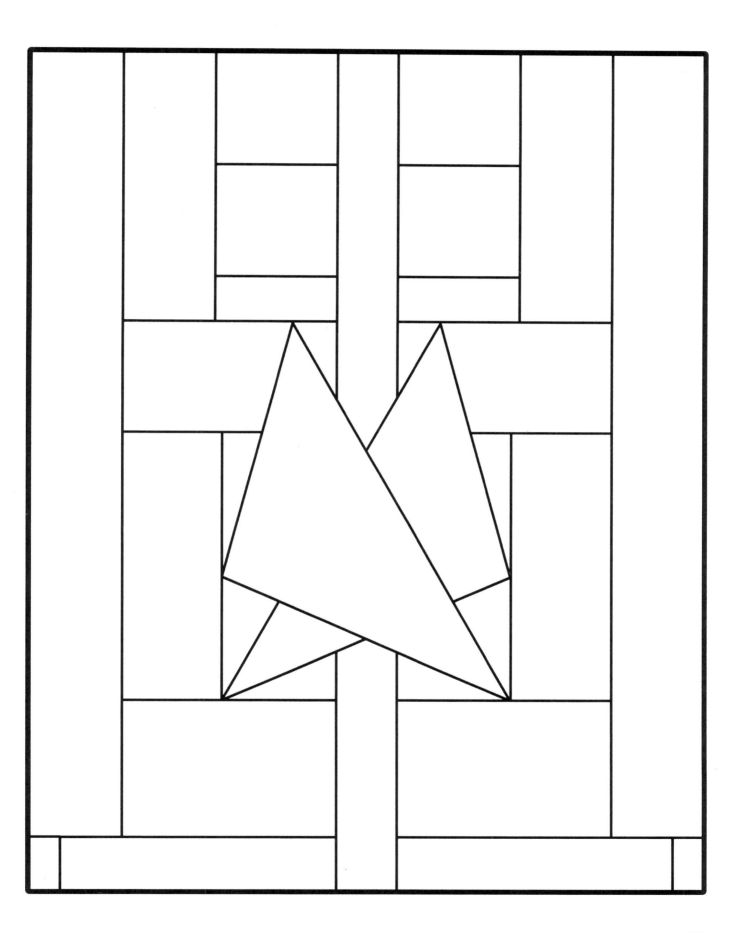

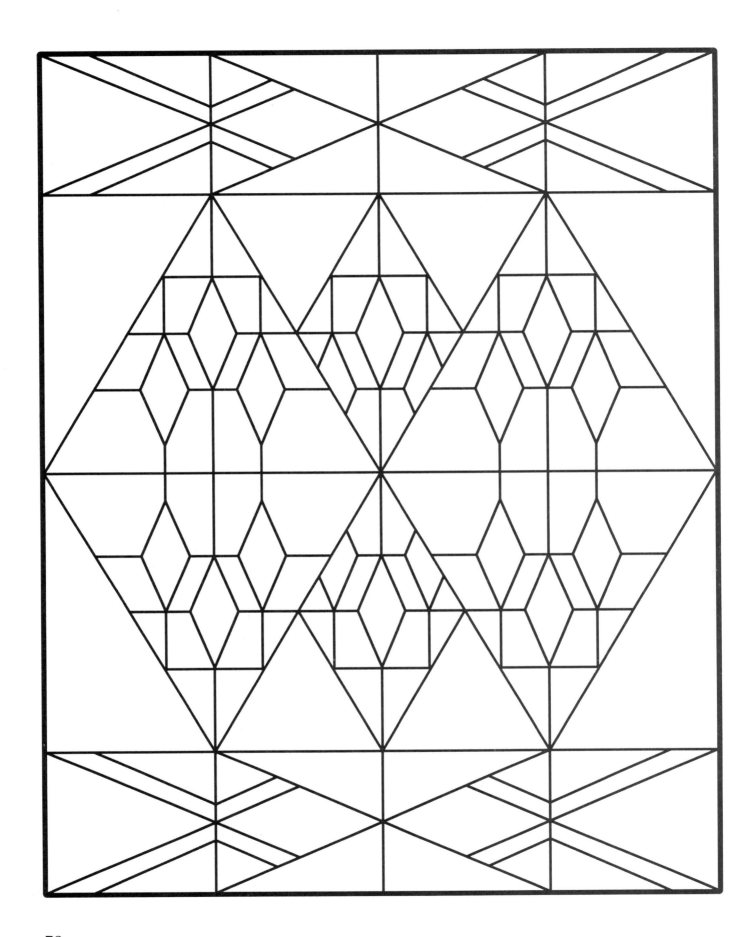

58

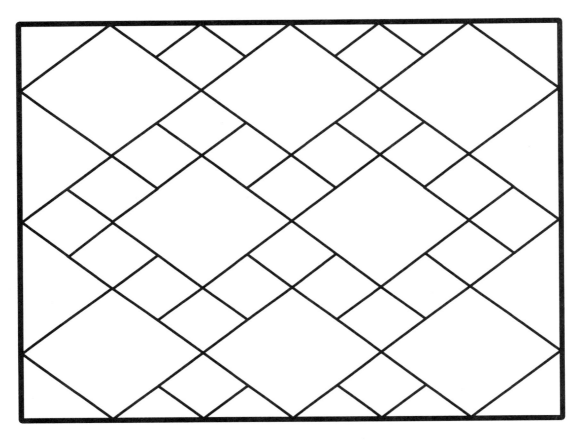

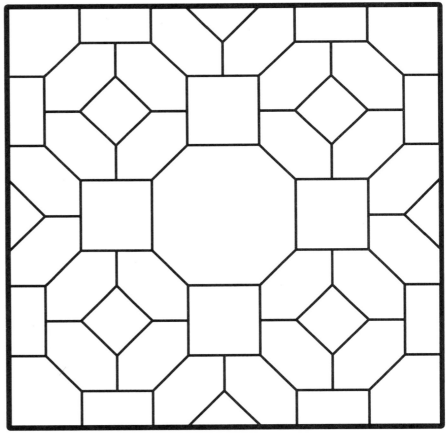

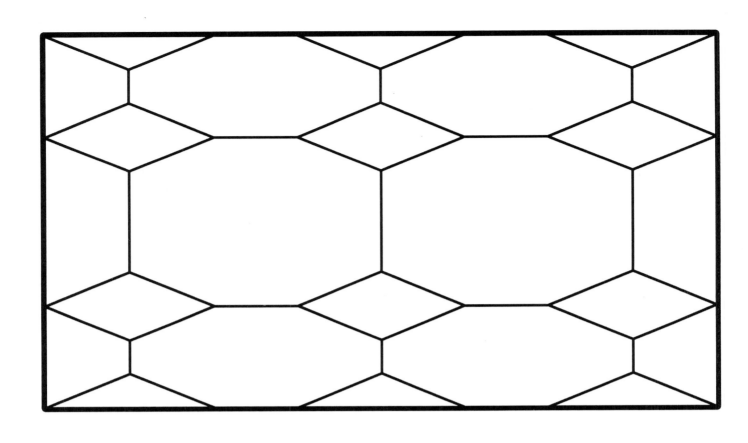

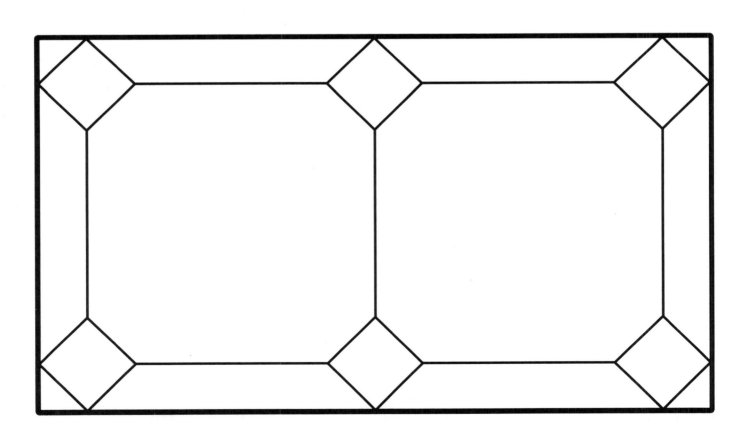

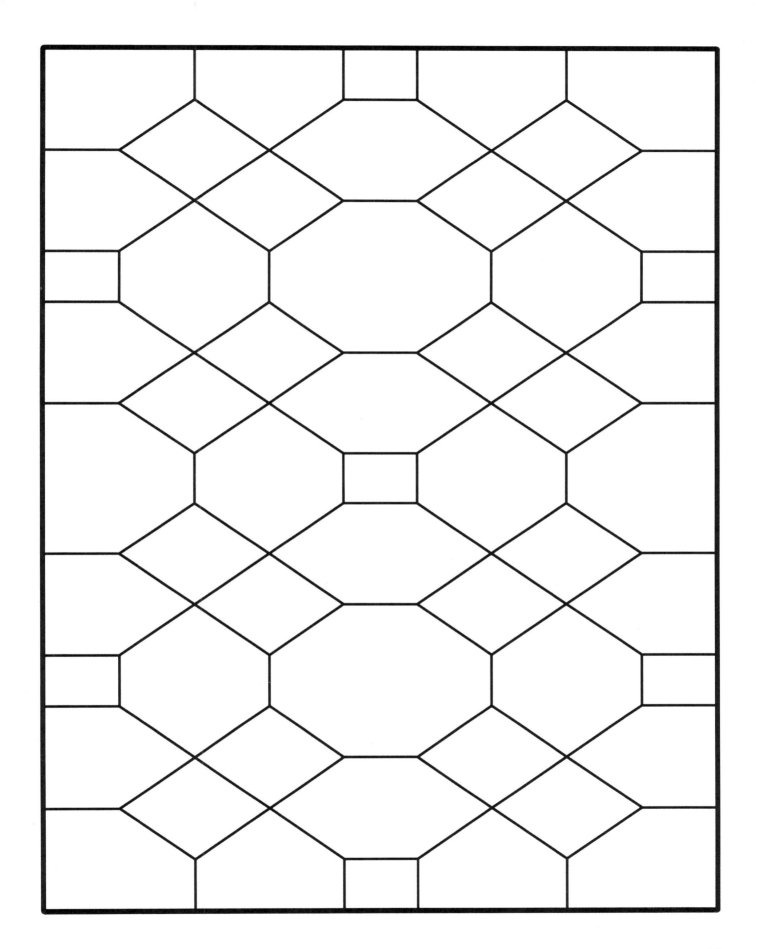

65

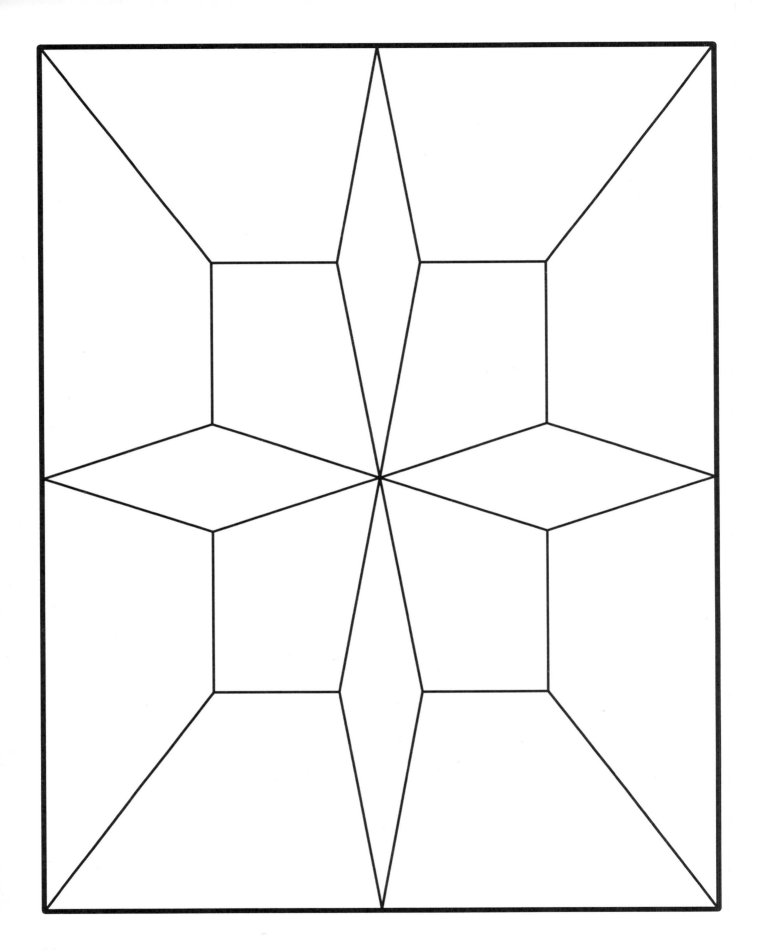

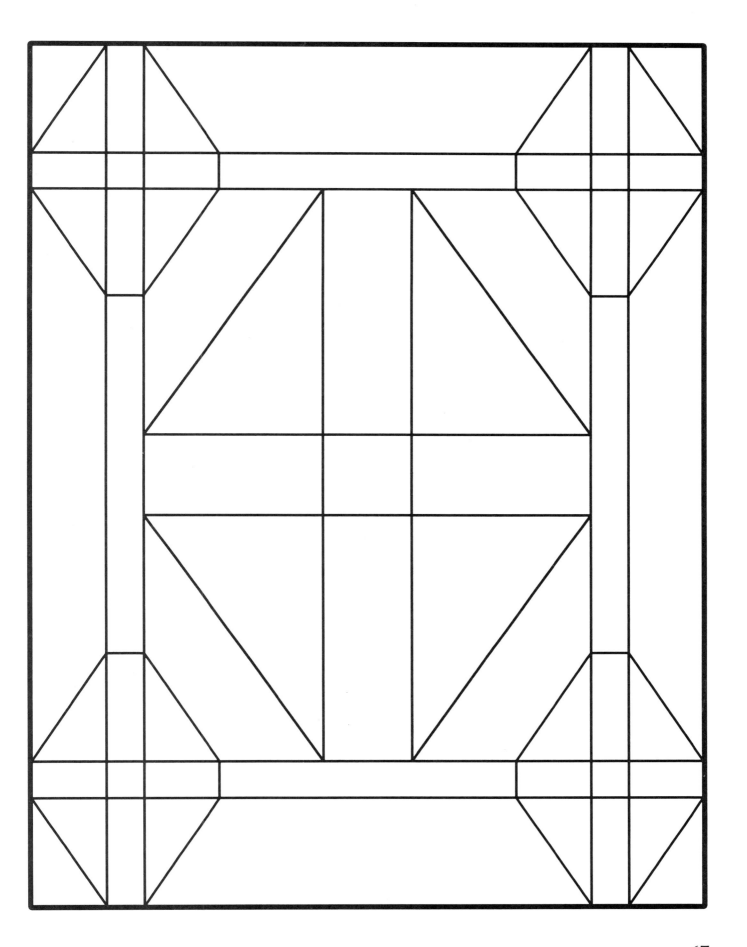

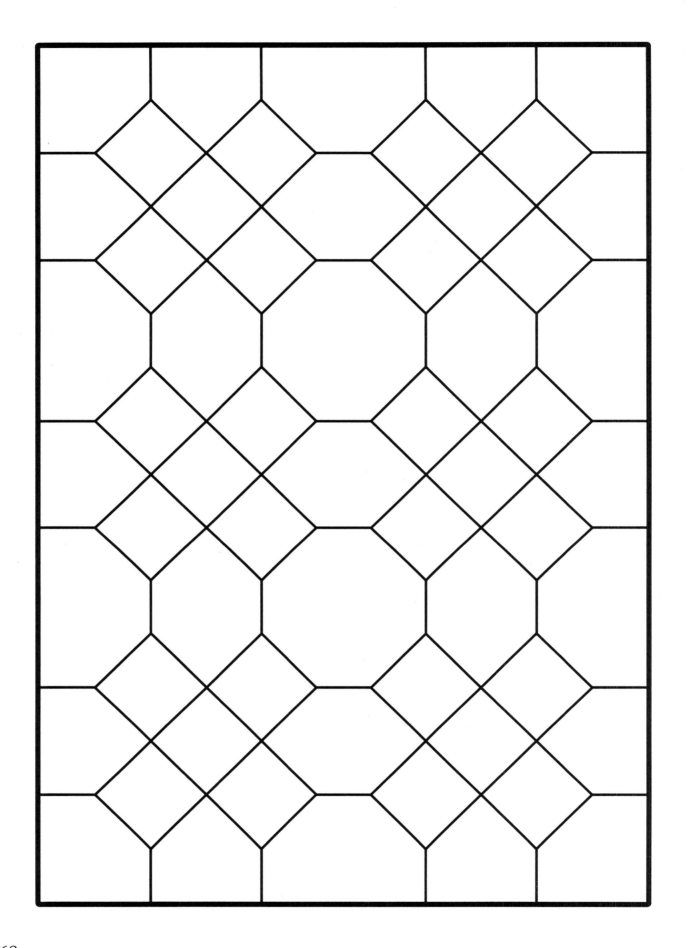

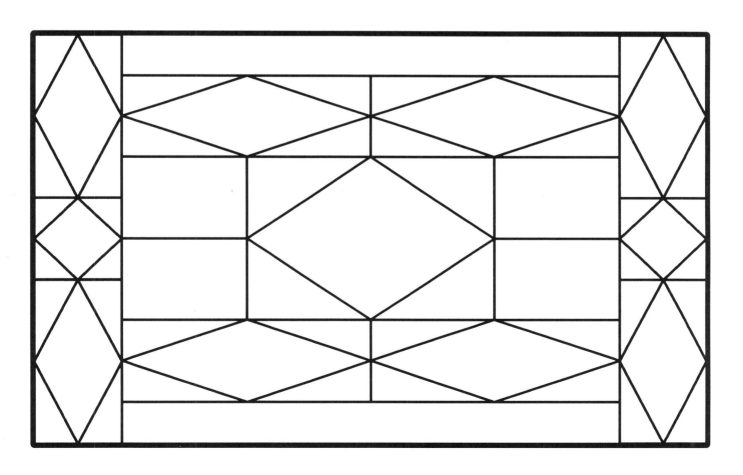

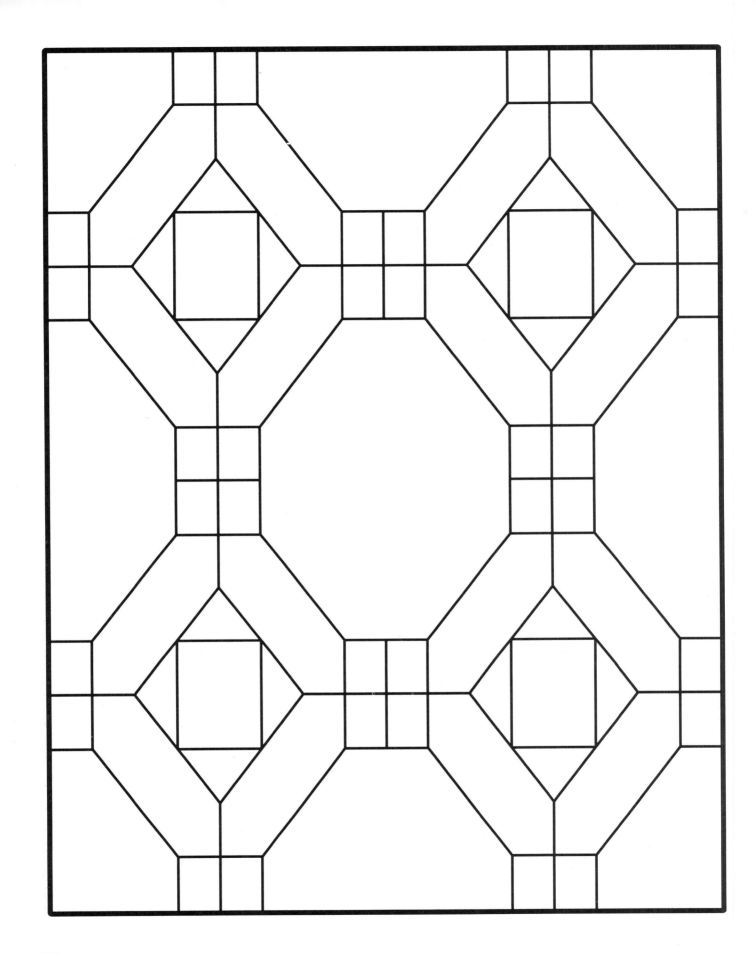

70

71

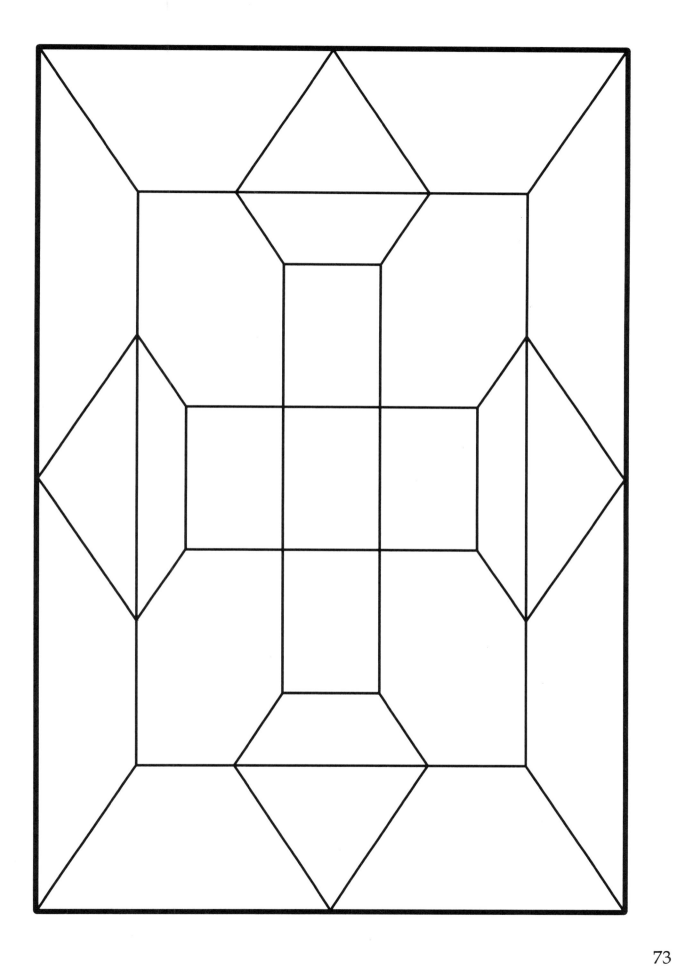

73

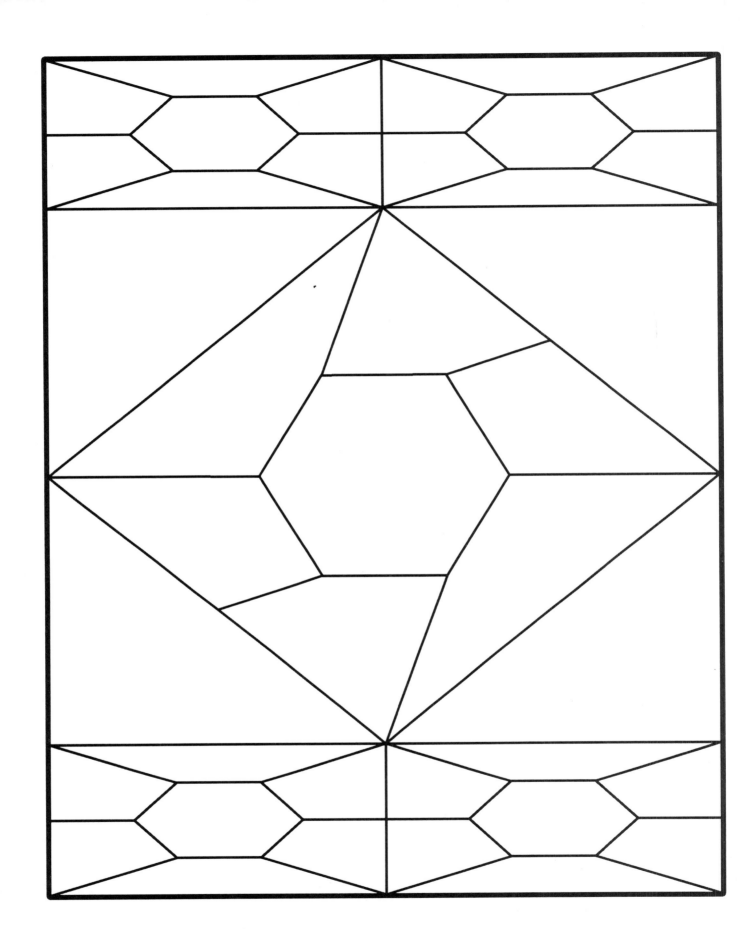

74

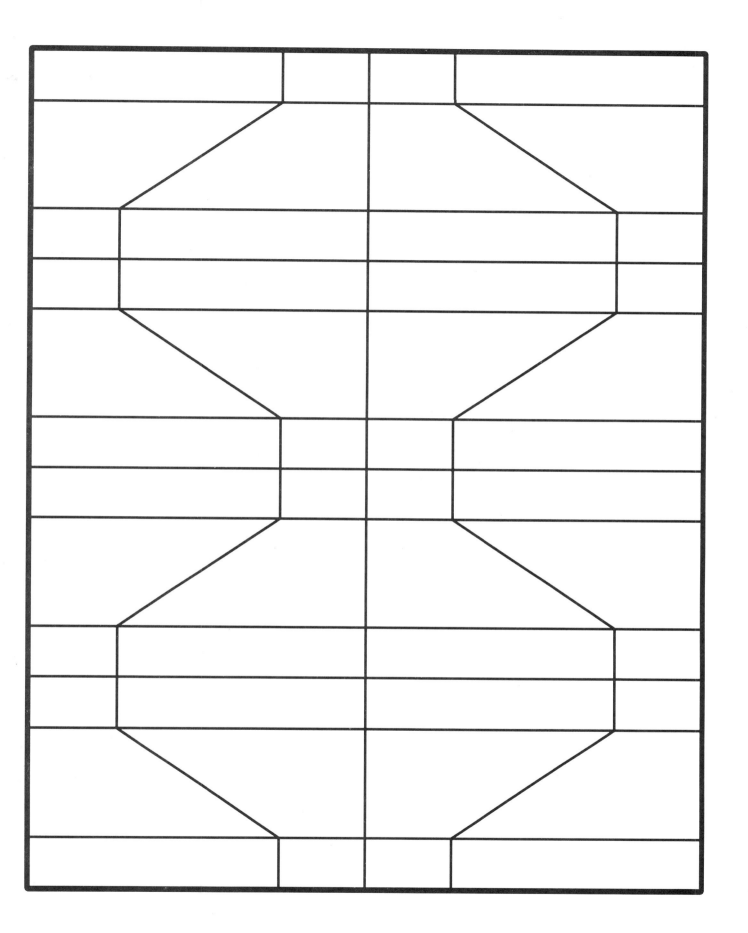

77

80

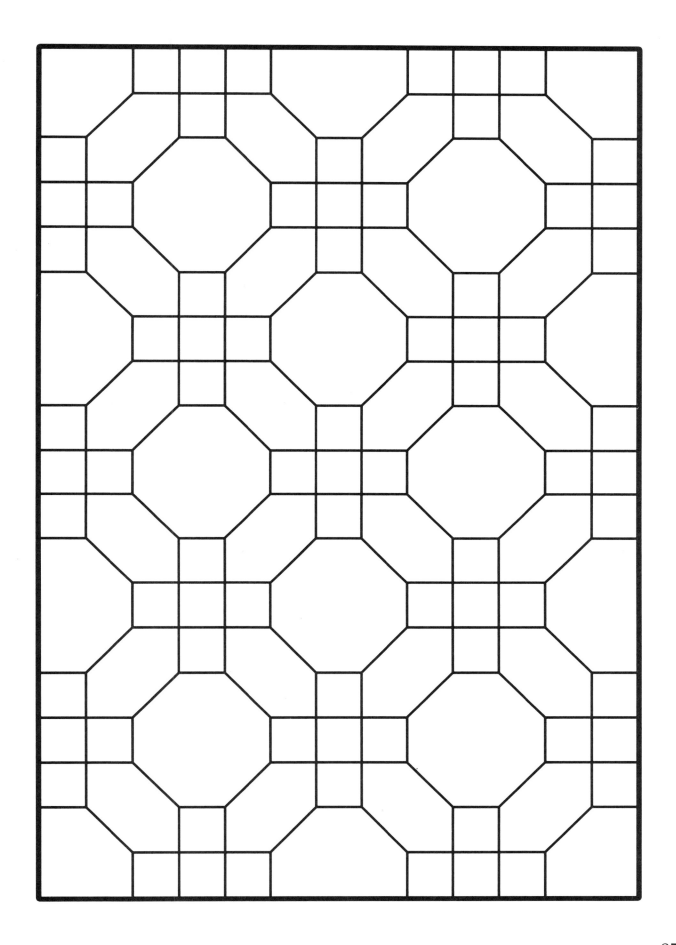

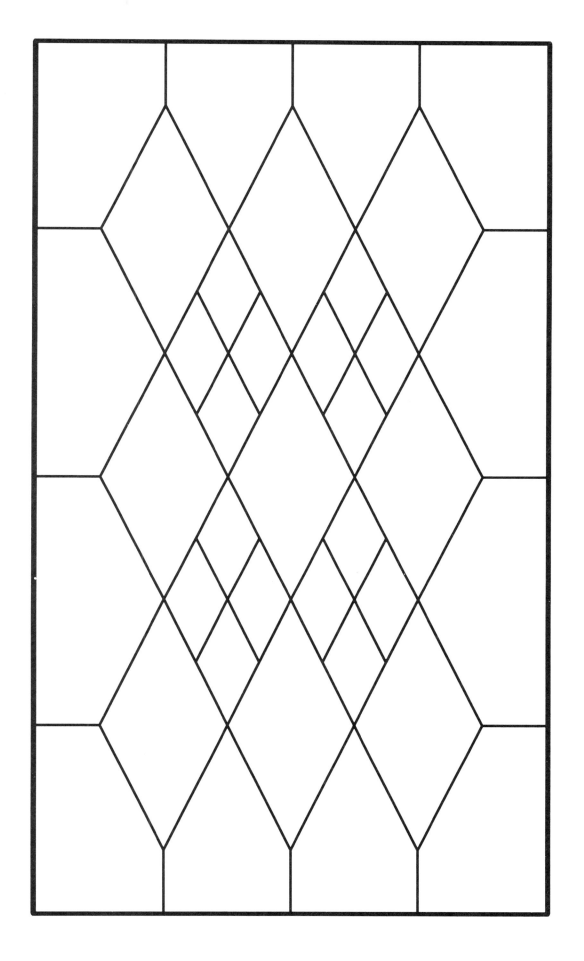

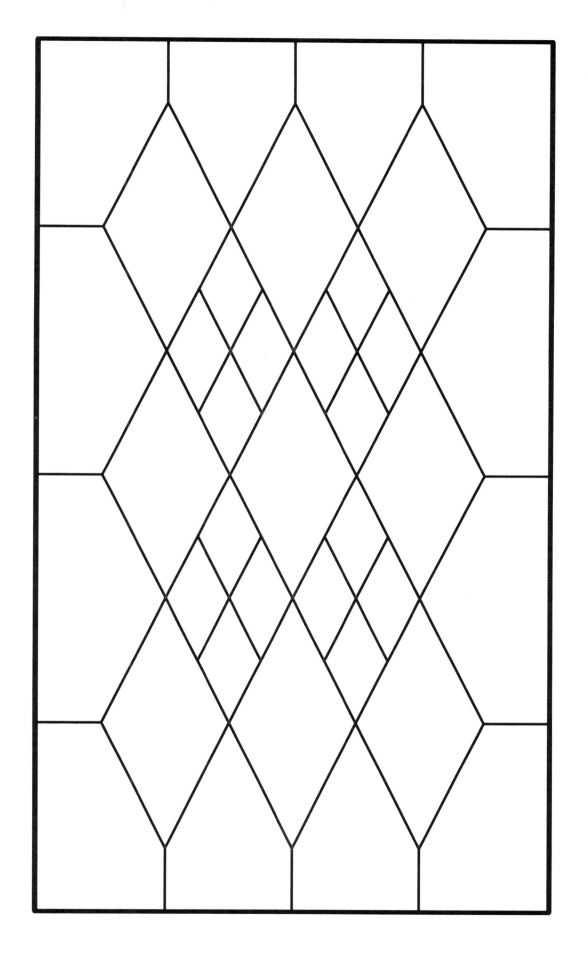

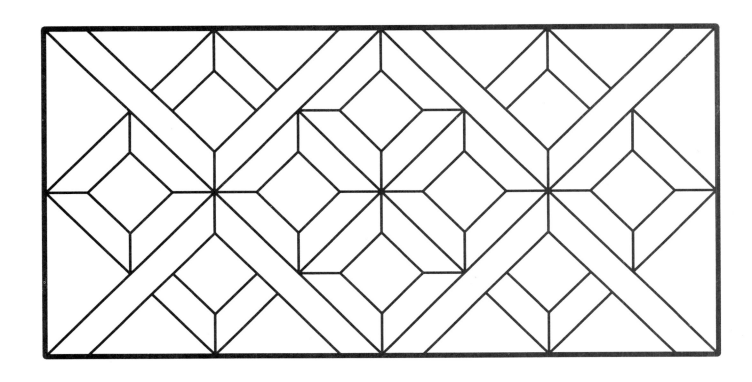

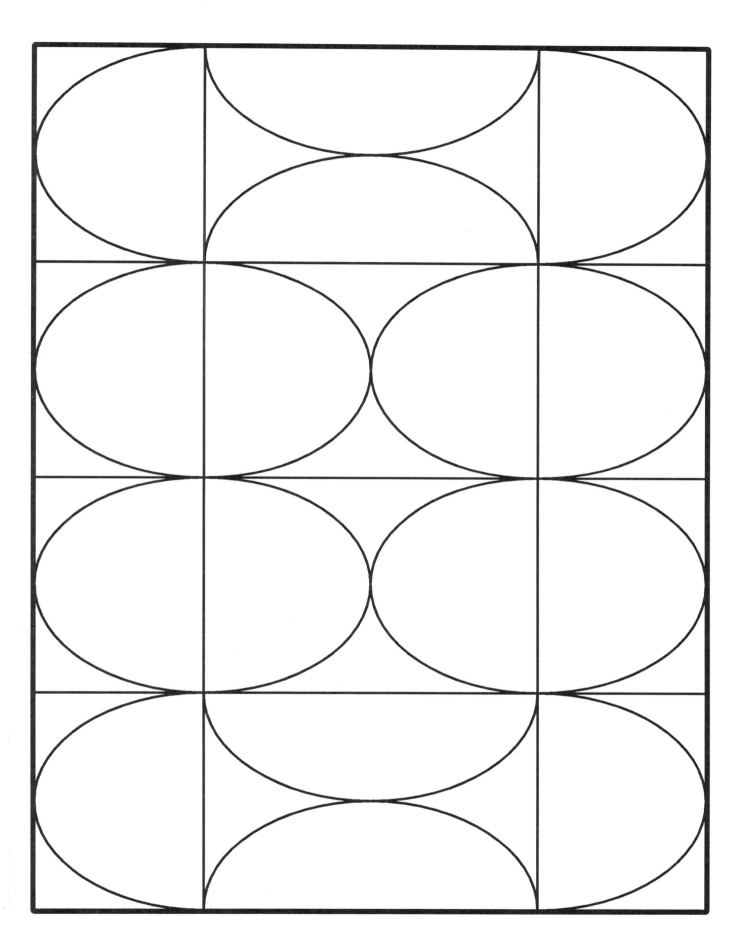

94

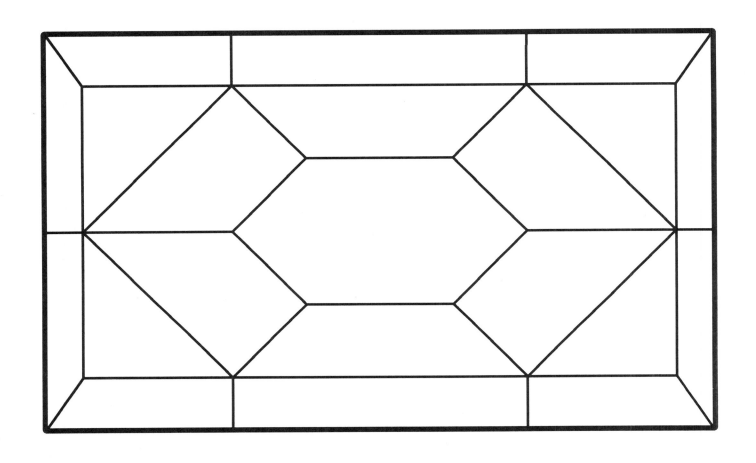

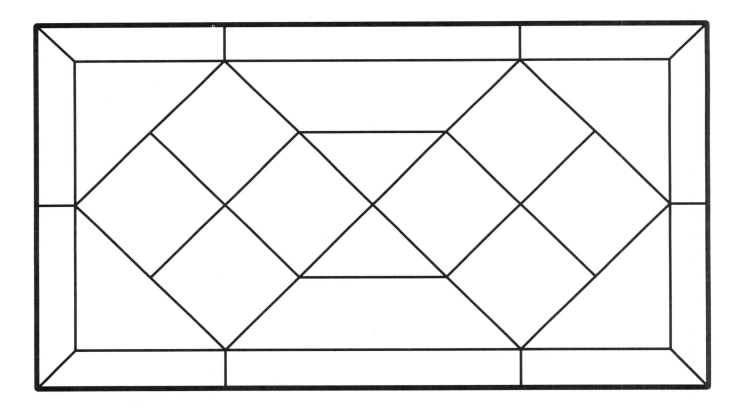

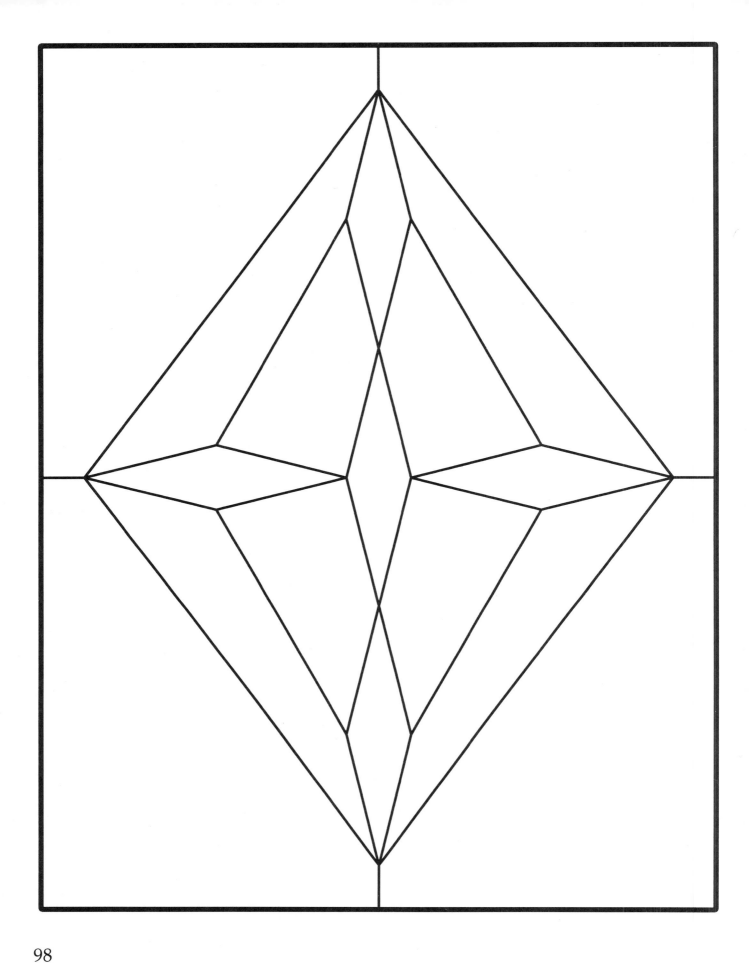

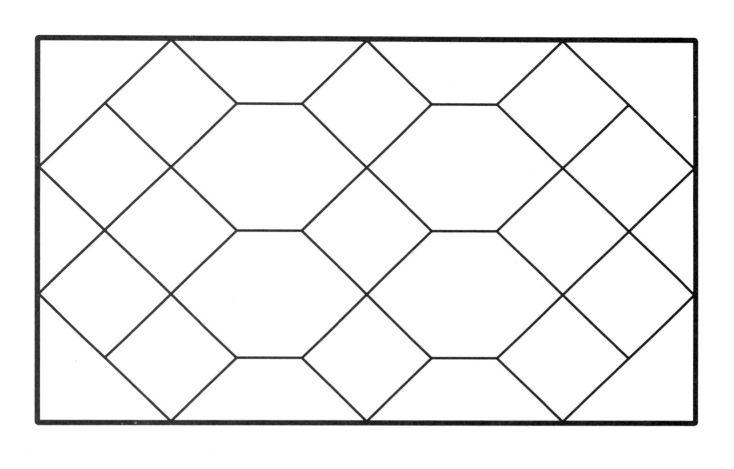

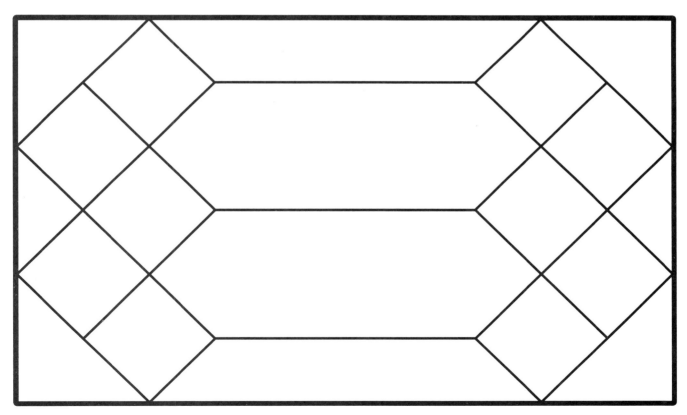

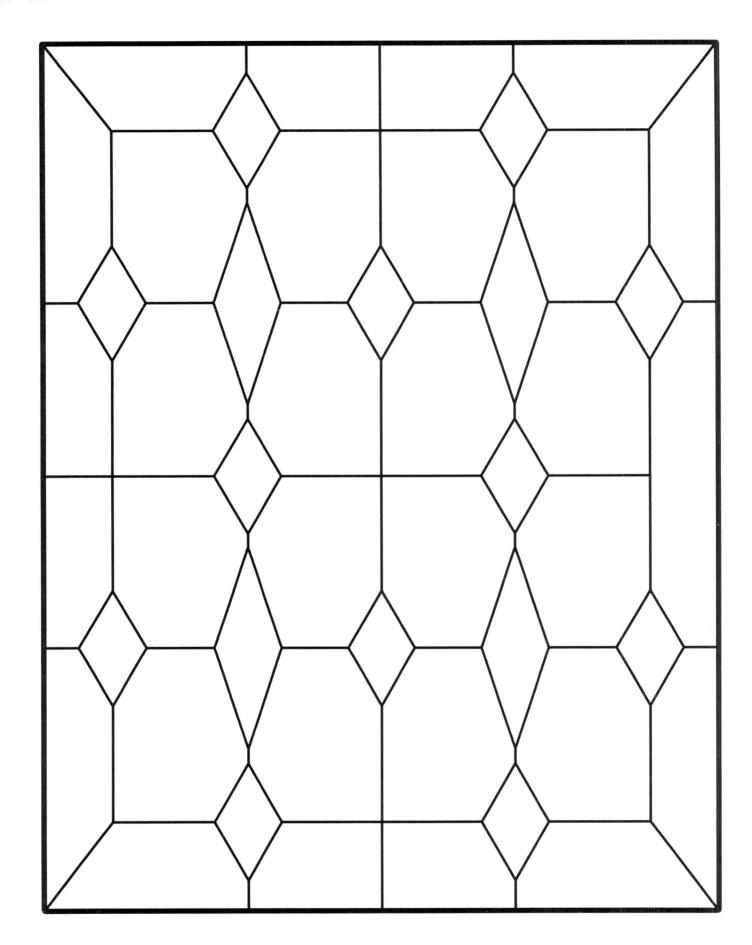

100

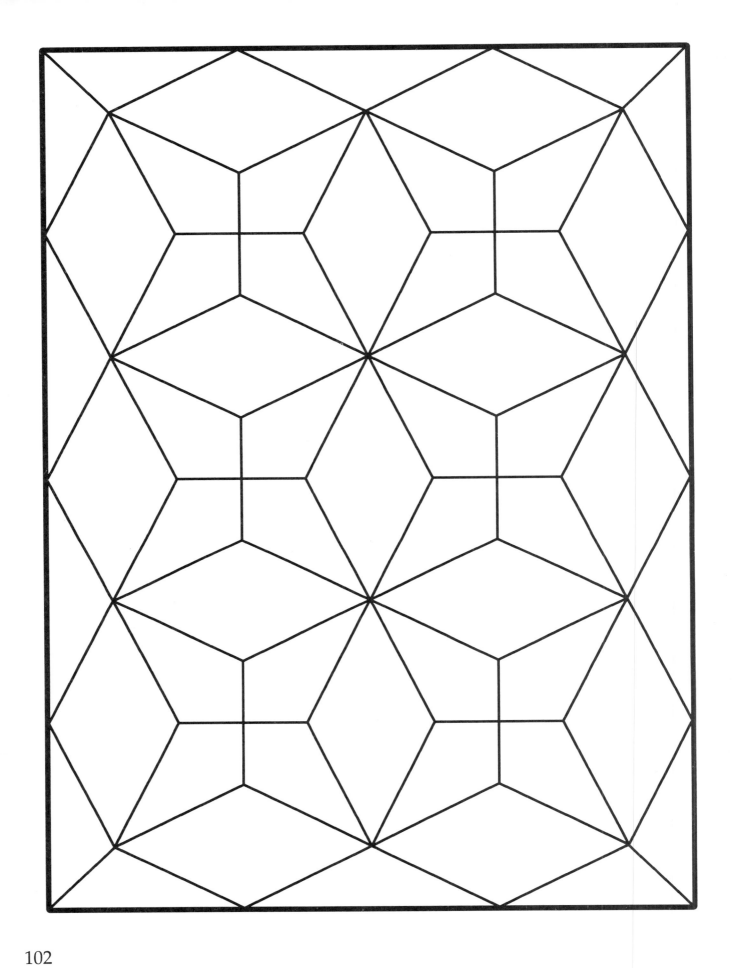

102

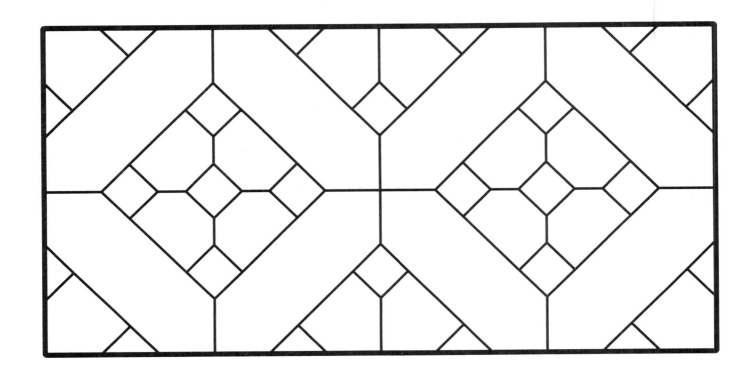

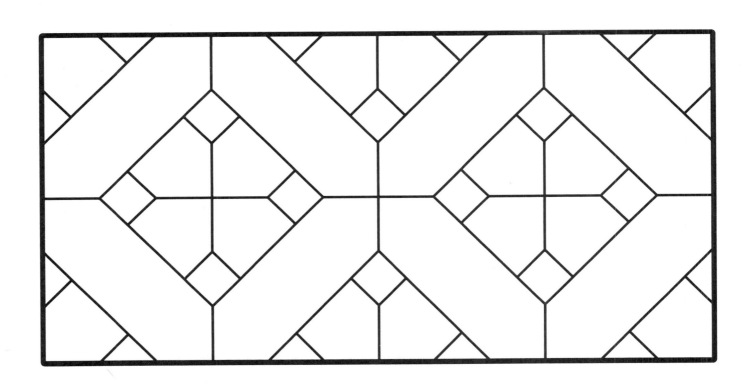

106

107

109

110

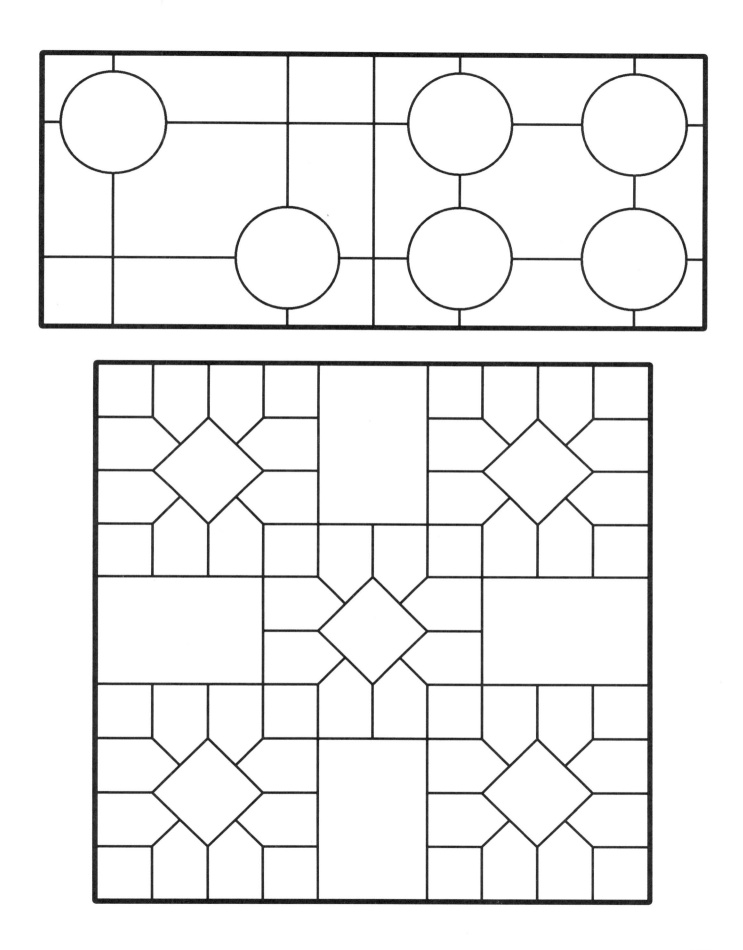

113

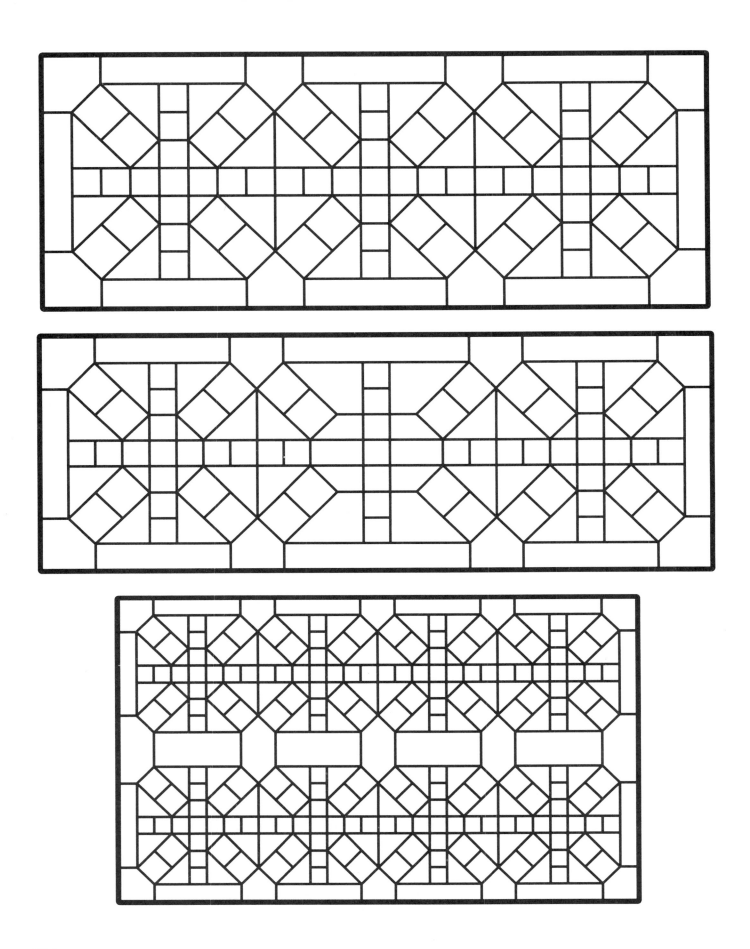

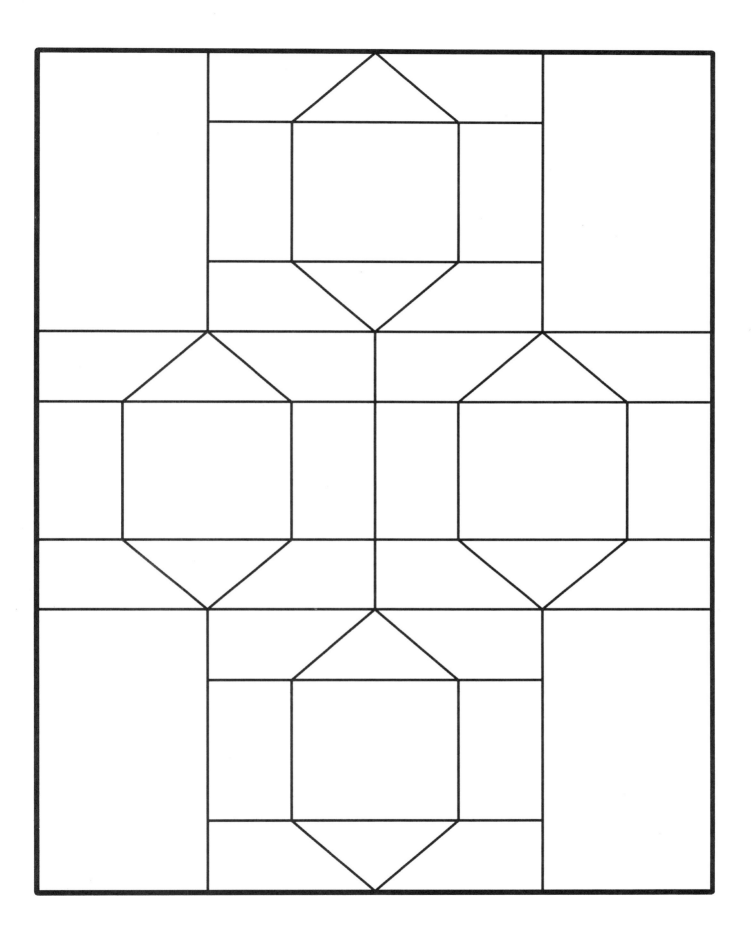

118

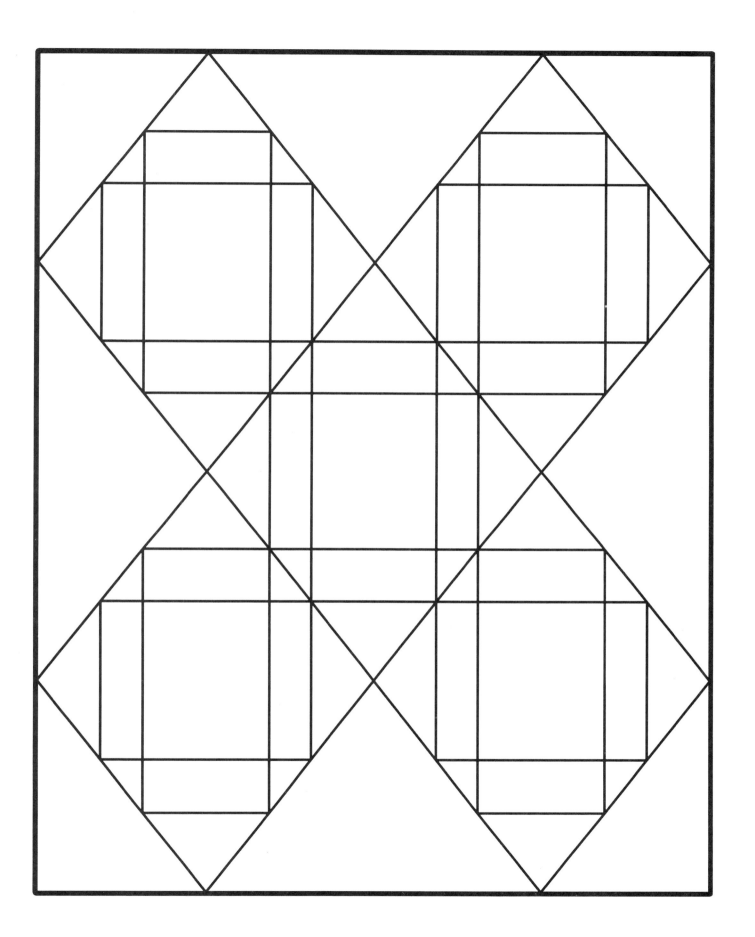

120